Twayne's English Authors Series

Sylvia E. Bowman, *Editor*
INDIANA UNIVERSITY

The *Pearl*-Poet

 64

THE *PEARL*-POET

by

CHARLES MOORMAN

Professor Moorman's book is the first critical work to deal exclusively with the works of an anonymous fourteenth-century author credited with the authorship of four striking poems — *Pearl*, an elegy on the death of the poet's daughter, *Purity*, a retelling of several Old Testament stories illustrating the virtue of chastity, *Patience*, a lively rendition of the tale of Jonah, and the popular *Sir Gawain and the Green Knight*, the best English Arthurian romance.

In dealing with the poems as a group rather than as individual poems, Mr. Moorman settles upon the moral and ethical issues dealt with by the poet as providing thematic unity within the poet's works, and demonstrates that the poet is everywhere concerned with the problem of man's disobedience to God's plan, and the impurity of life which stems from that disobedience.

In the course of this examination, Mr. Moorman is careful to review the various theories of authorship, source material, and purpose which have dominated the previous work on the *Pearl*-poet. Where they are necessary to an understanding of the poet, medieval concepts, especially those of theology and chivalry, have been explained.

The Pearl-*Poet* thus provides a much-needed general introduction to the works of an author who is, next to Chaucer, the most widely-ready English author of the fourteenth century.

The *Pearl*-Poet

By Charles Moorman
University of *Southern Mississippi*

Twayne Publishers, Inc.   ::   New York

For GEOFFREY and STELLA MUMFORD

ABOUT THE AUTHOR

Charles Moorman was born in Cincinnati, Ohio, in 1925 and was educated in the public schools of Covington, Kentucky. After serving in the Armed Forces in World War II, he attended Kenyon College where he received the A.B. degree with High Honors in English in 1949. He received his M.A. and Ph.D. degrees from Tulane University in 1951 and 1953. In 1954 he joined the faculty of the University of Southern Mississippi where since 1956 he has been Professor of English and Chairman of the Department of English. He spent 1960-61 as a Guggenheim Fellow and 1964-5 as a Fellow of the American Council of Learned Societies in England.

Mr. Moorman is the author of over thirty articles in learned journals on various aspects of medieval and modern literature, particularly the Arthurian legend. His books include *Arthurian Triptych*, *The Book of Kyng Arthur*, *The Precincts of Felicity*, and *A Knyght There Was*. He is currently at work on an edition of the *Pearl*-poet and on a book on love and fortune in *The Canterbury Tales*.

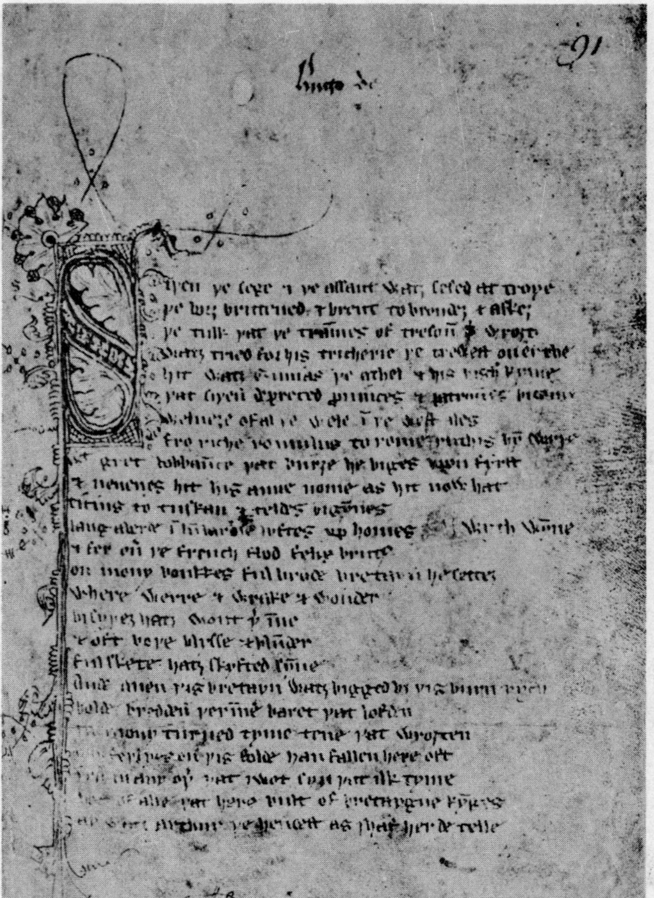

THE *PEARL*-POET

Preface

The following study is intended as a general introduction to one of the great English poets, the so-called *Pearl-* or *Gawain-*poet, who flourished in the latter part of the fourteenth century. His works are all contained in a single manuscript which is on display in the British Museum and which is still designated by the catalogue reference number—Cotton Nero A.x.—that it bore in the library of the eminent seventeenth-century bibliophile Sir Robert Cotton, who arranged his volumes in cases under the busts of Roman emperors.

The manuscript itself is a small, bound quarto (7 x 5 inches) written in a single sharp scribal hand (though with corrections in a second hand); and it contains in addition to the four poems attributed to the *Pearl-*poet, two Latin texts. The manuscript is now faded, and many of the lines can be read only by means of their "offset" images on the backs of the pages opposite. The poems themselves are untitled (their present titles were given to them by modern editors) and are arranged in the order of *Pearl*, *Purity* (sometimes called *Cleanness*), *Patience,* and *Sir Gawain and the Green Knight.* The manuscript also contains a number of illustrations of scenes in the text.

The language and style of the poems indicate that the *Pearl-*poet was a native of the north-west Midlands of England, probably of Lancashire, a region remote in the fourteenth century from the rapidly changing climate of life in London. He thus lived through the tumultuous era of Richard II, though his work shows little interest either in politics or in the profound social forces at work in late Plantagenet England. He was also a contemporary of Geoffrey Chaucer, though his provincial language, his meter, and his theological and moral interests are sharply different from the more sophisticated style and themes of the London-born Chaucer. The work of the *Pearl-*poet is in fact a part of the great fourteenth-century Northern revival of alliterative poetry which includes such poems as *Wynnere and Wastoure* and *The Parlement of the Thre Ages* and which has as its greatest monument *Piers Plowman*. Alliterative Revival poetry is conservative in its characteristic use of the accentual meters of Old English verse rather than of the syllabic measures which had come to England with the Norman invaders; in its rejection of French courtliness in favor of a strict code of morality; in its repeated demands for social and ecclesiastical reform; and in its glorification of the native English countryside, a landscape very near to that which Wordsworth celebrated four-hundred years later. Though the *Pearl*-poet is seemingly very little interested in reform, he does share in great measure the other characteristics of the school; and it is principally as a moral poet, though never as a merely didactic one, that this study intends to present him.

Like most medieval literature, these four poems present almost insuperable problems. For example, there is no general agreement among scholars as to the precise dialect employed by the poet, the exact region or time of composition, the identity, the occupation, or the social status of the poet, or even the theological and social ideas the poet held or the literary genres and modes of composition he employed. But, although these difficulties exist, it would be folly to let them stand, as they often are permitted to do, between the reader and the poems. Scholarly analyses of publication, biography, authenticity, attribution, chronology, tradition, influence, and sources—although clear in intent—have in actual practice difficult rules of procedure; and, all too often, the game of scholarship itself assumes an importance greater than that of its object—the illumination of a literary text.

It can be assumed, I think, that the general reader to whom this volume is addressed has some familiarity with these techniques, and hence there is no need here to explain them. However, recent medieval criticism has developed three approaches so specialized as to necessitate some explanation. The first of these, the application of the symbols and narrative patterns of myth and folklore to the text, derives largely from the ritual studies of Sir James Frazer, Jane Harrison, Gilbert Murray, and the other Cambridge anthropologists of the early twentieth century, all of whom regarded myth as the spoken correlative of the first rituals of primitive man. The great ancient myths of creation and fertility in all cultures are thus said to contain the earliest concrete embodiments of a store of universally repeated patterns of life and thought, of concepts and themes which lie very close to the basic concerns of all men in all ages, to their highest aspirations and most secret terrors. The discovery of mythical elements within a formal work of literature thus allows the critic to recognize its essential meaning.

A great number of medievalists, such as W. A. Nitze, A. H. Krappe, Jessie L. Weston, and John Speirs, have searched for and found in medieval literature echoes of Celtic and Germanic myth; and, in spite of occasional excesses of subtlety, they have succeeded in revealing layer after layer of meaning in works whose surfaces had long been impervious to more routine methods of attack.

The second technique, patristical exegesis, is more recent and more controversial than myth application. The basic theory, held principally by D. W. Robertson, Jr., Bernard F. Huppé, and Robert E. Kaske, holds that "all serious poetry written by Christians during the Middle Ages promotes the doctrine of charity by using the same allegorical structure that the [early Church] Fathers found in the Bible." [1] The method is thus an attempt to establish the particular literary use made of biblical allusions by determining from a close reading of the glosses of the early commentators their exact significance to medieval people. The value of this technique is obvious in works such as *Piers Plowman* and *Pearl*, where the religious theme of the work quite naturally entails a considerable use of Scripture by their authors. The potential worth of the method in revealing layers of meaning clear to medieval people but lost to us, however, as well as its highly controversial status, can best be observed in its application to such a secular piece as Chaucer's "Miller's Tale," where a stratum of biblical allusion promoting the theme of charity would hardly be expected. [2]

The third special method, iconology, is still in its infancy, but it bids fair to become the most valuable of the three. Like patristical exegesis, iconographical study is an attempt to recover that most illusive will-o'-the-wisp, the medieval "point of view," this time through a thorough searching of all the medieval arts. "Just as medieval art developed certain conventional ways of indicating the identity of a saint, the character of a vice, or the ramifi-

cations of an idea represented by a pagan deity, medieval literature developed a conventional language of narrative or descriptive
motifs which were designed to communicate ideas." [3] Thus D. W.
Robertson's *Preface to Chaucer* contains over a hundred plates
illustrating in art and sculpture iconographical representations of
concepts which appear in Chaucer's poetry. Like the use of
biblical allusion, the application of the icons of art to the images
of literature can do much to reveal themes and layers of meaning
in medieval literature which its first audiences readily understood
but which have been lost with the passing of time and the
changes of custom.

As a general introduction to the *Pearl*-poet, this book is not
committed to any one approach, but makes use of a variety of
techniques in order to fulfill a two-fold purpose—to present a
comprehensive and coherent view of each of the four poems in
order to illuminate its special themes and values and, at the same
time, to designate those ideas and techniques that characterize
the four poems as a group. Each chapter thus follows the organizational scheme demanded by the subject matter and by those
critical approaches most suitable to it, but each discusses the
problems common to all the poems—the place of the poem in the
author's general development, its structure, and its specific
themes. Chapter 2, devoted to *Pearl*, is mainly structural and
philosophical in emphasis, treating the poem principally as a
beautifully articulated elegy. The chapters on *Patience* and
Purity are, as they must be, almost wholly structural and theological in nature. Chapter 5 on the other hand, which deals with
Sir Gawain and the Green Knight, is much more general than the
preceding chapters, though it does deal extensively with the
structural use of myth in the poem, an approach which here
seems to best reveal the heart of the poem.

Chapter 1 is an account of the major problems surrounding the
whole group of poems—their authorship, chronology, diction,
geographical origin—all those factors, in short, which bind the
poems together and establish them as the canon of a single fourteenth-century literary genius. Chapter 6 provides a natural conclusion, just as Chapter 1 provides a natural beginning; for here
the poet's total work is summed up in terms of his general themes
and his uses of the literary devices known to him.

In discussing the poems, it will be necessary to summarize the results of the hundred years of scholarship expended on them since their publication in modern times. Needless to say, not every opinion can be considered or even noted, though I hope that the major theories are adequately covered. Nor does this book attempt to solve the many complex problems of meaning which arise from almost every line of the text or to advance any radically original interpretations. Where disagreements among the masters exist, I have pointed them out; and I have everywhere tried to distinguish between fact and conjecture.

Some readers may note also that I nowhere touch upon the possibility of the *Pearl*-poet's having written also *St. Erkenwald,* a fourteenth-century alliterative poem, written probably in London, that recounts a miracle attributed to a bishop. The evidence for such an attribution is exceedingly slim,[4] and the unity of this study would be severely disturbed by including for serious consideration a very doubtful part of the poet's canon.

My ultimate aim, however, is not simply to summarize the work done on the poems or to point up their excellences of technique and form or even to attempt to fix authoritatively their themes and meanings. My major objective is to introduce them as old and valued friends to a new group of readers and to reintroduce them to those readers who once met them casually, but have since forgotten the introduction. If this volume thus causes the reader to look into *Sir Gawain and the Green Knight* or *Pearl* for the first time or to pull down his sophomore anthology for a second, more careful, look at the poems, it will have succeeded in its principal aim—even though the reader's reaction might well be to reject what my book has to say in favor of his own insights. Like the physician, the critic anticipates the time at which his services will be no longer needed.

The bibliography which concludes the volume is of necessity highly selective. The translations in the text are by various hands.

CHARLES MOORMAN

University of Southern Mississippi

Acknowledgments

Portions of Chapters 2 and 3 of this work appeared originally in the following articles: "The Role of the Narrator in *Pearl*," *Modern Philology* (November, 1955) and "The Role of the Narrator in *Patience*," *Modern Philology* (November, 1963) and are reprinted from *Modern Philology* by permission of the University of Chicago Press, copyright 1955 and 1963 by The University of Chicago.

The lines from the translations of *Patience* from *Romance, Vision and Satire* by Jessie L. Weston and *Pearl* by Sophie Jewett are reprinted by permission of their publishers, Houghton Mifflin Company and Thomas Y. Crowell Company. The translations from *Sir Gawain and the Green Knight* are taken from *Sir Gawain and the Green Knight* translated by Theodore Howard Banks, Jr., copyright, 1929, by F. S. Crofts and Co., Inc., and are reprinted by permission of Appleton-Century-Crofts, Division of Meredith Publishing Company.

I am grateful to Miss Perry Lou Milner, who typed the manuscript several times, to Dr. Sylvia E. Bowman, who all too often saved me from my unconsidered enthusiasm for the *Pearl*-poet, and, as always, to my wife Ruth, without whose unfailing understanding and encouragement I would never have written a word.

Contents

Chronology

1327–77	Reign of Edward III.
1322	Birth of William Langland, the author of *Piers Plowman,* the most important of the Alliterative Revival poems.
ca. 1340	Birth of Geoffrey Chaucer.
1345	The founding of the Order of the Garter, the motto of which appears in *Sir Gawain and the Green Knight.*
1346	The Battle of Crécy.
1348	The first great scourge of the Black Death.
1351	The Statute of Laborers which attempted to restrict the wages of serfs.
ca. 1352	*Wynnere and Wastoure,* one of the important poems of the Alliterative Revival.
1356	The Battle of Poitiers.
ca. 1356	The publication of Mandeville's *Travels,* one of the sources of *Purity.*
ca. 1360–1390	The flourishing of the *Pearl*-poet.
1360	Boccaccio's *Olympia,* one of the sources of *Pearl.*
ca. 1360	The Alliterative *Morte Darthur,* one of the last Arthurian romances in English.
1362	The A-text or first version of *Piers Plowman.*
ca. 1370	*The Book of the Duchess,* Chaucer's first important work.
1376	The death of the Black Prince, the eldest son of Edward III.
1377	The B-text of *Piers Plowman,* parts of which seem to echo passages in *Patience.*
1377–99	Reign of Richard II.
1381	The Peasants' Revolt.
1385	The Wyclif Bible.

ca. 1385	*Troilus and Criseyde,* Chaucer's longest and most important narrative poem.
1385–1400	The period of composition of Chaucer's *Canterbury Tales.*
1390	John Gower's *Confessio Amantis.*
ca. 1395	The C-text of *Piers Plowman.*
1399–1413	Reign of Henry IV.
1400	The death of Chaucer.
ca. 1400	The date of the *Pearl*-poet manuscript.

CHAPTER 1

The Anonymous Poet

ENGLAND in the last years of the fourteenth century was embroiled, somewhat prematurely, in the transition of Europe from the Middle Ages to the Renaissance. The increasing corruption within the Church, the rising power of Parliament following the signing of Magna Carta, the unsteady throne, and the effect of the plagues upon the economic status of the serf and hence upon the whole economic basis of fourteenth-century society gave rise to a profound series of changes in the political and social life of England.

The late fourteenth century was in every way a century of contrasting and shifting values. It marked the breakdown of the firm Catholic world order and the unity of medieval social, political, and religious thought, and it saw the beginnings of the rise of nationalism and religious dispersion. It witnessed the passage from manor and village to town life and the rise of the middle class, and it marked the shift from feudalism to constitutional monarchy. It was the age of the mystic Dame Juliana of Norwich and of Jean Froissart, the chronicler of chivalry; but it was also the age of the religious reformer John Wyclif and of the Peasants' Revolt. The fourteenth century was caught in the struggle of the centripetal forces of the old theocratic order with the centrifugal drive of the new nationalism and the vanguard of the Reformation. The *Pearl*-poet lived, though no chronicler could have told him so, in the twilight of the Middle Ages.

Actually, however, the seeds of England's problems in the fourteenth century were sown three hundred years previously by the Norman invaders of 1066. The Battle of Hastings was as decisive as it was brief; and, although the conquering Norman lords made no serious efforts to disperse the Saxons as the Saxons had themselves dispersed the Celts in the fifth and sixth centuries, they quickly established themselves as masters of the island. The

Tower of London, built by William I, proclaimed to the city of
London, as did the new Romanesque castles and cathedrals all
over England, the supremacy of the French masters over their
new subjects.

Nor were William's efforts directed towards subduing the Saxons simply as a show of his great power. The practical mind of
the Conqueror was quick to understand local conditions and to
frame such laws as were needed to insure peace and to bring to
England the same system of government he had managed so
efficiently in France—Norman feudalism. The hated Doomsday
Book, ordered by William, in which were recorded the status and
whereabouts of every man, ox, and plow in England, became the
basis of William's land allocation and taxation and hence of his
control over the country he had conquered.

By the end of the Anglo-Saxon period, most of England's present forty shires, or counties as they were called after 1066, had
been formed. These shires had developed from the gradual fusing
of small, autonomous kingdoms, and each of them had been
largely self-sufficient under the rule of its "ealdorman" and its local courts, the "moots." The shires were in turn divided into "hun-
dreds" and "townships," each of which was, like the shire, almost
totally self-governing. There was a king, of course, and from the
reign of King Alfred in the late ninth century, considerable royal
influence. But there was nothing in Saxon England that even re-
motely resembled the strong, centralized dukedoms of France.

The shift in government and in the theory of it that William
brought displaced almost entirely the Anglo-Saxon autocracy, the
thanes and the high churchmen; and it replaced the highest level
of Saxon government with military and manorial feudalism. William, as was the custom, kept for himself a "demesne" or royal
domain and delegated the remainder of the country as "fiefs" to
his closest military supporters, themselves of course noblemen, in
return for which they swore to be his loyal "vassals," to render
him both "homage" and "fealty," and to lend him as part of a
precise, though complex, system of "aids" and "relief," financial
and military support. These noblemen in turn established their
demesnes and apportioned land to their vassals, thus knitting the
lords of the country at all levels by bonds of financial and military responsibility.

Although William was content to leave local self-government

largely untampered with, he was careful to keep the ultimate power in England under his own close control. He limited the power of the English earldoms by refusing to grant to any of his vassals large parcels of land in a single area, and in time he demanded that all landholders, even the lower vassals, pledge their military allegiance to him rather than to their immediate overlords. There thus grew up among the barons during the hundred years following the invasion a resentment against the increasing power of their Plantagenet rulers, a resentment culminating in the barons' assertion of their prerogatives in Magna Carta and, more importantly for our study of the *Pearl*-poet, in the rift between the North-country barons and the London-court aristocracy in the so-called "baronial opposition" of the fourteenth century.[1]

I *After 1066*

The lasting effects of the Norman invasion were not all in the sphere of government. The Normans brought to England the French language and a culture far more sophisticated than that of the Anglo-Saxons. But the extreme stratification of social classes in Anglo-Norman Britain prevented for two hundred years any considerable amalgamation of the two languages and cultures. Latin, even more than before the invasion, became the official language of both Church and state; and French was the only language spoken at court or among the ruling classes everywhere, while English was relegated to the status of a peasant tongue. The monarchs of England immediately following the invasion knew no English whatsoever, nor would there have been any purpose in their bothering to learn the language. And even though there is a firm tradition of literature in English beginning in the thirteenth century, not until 1399 did an English king speak to Parliament in English. As Sir Walter Scott notes in *Ivanhoe*, English is the only language to have two terms for the common domestic animals: the Saxon peasant slaughtered "pigs," "cows," and "sheep"; the Norman lord ate "porc," "boeuf," and "mouton." And into the areas remote from London, the growing elegance and charm of the French invader's court hardly penetrated.

Yet despite the gradual amalgamation of language and culture and the emergence of a new nation and tradition in the years leading up to the Hundred Years' War, some separation of Briton and Norman apparently remained in the remote recesses of the

Northern and Western counties and especially in the earldoms of
Arundel, Warwick, and Hereford. Here the great baronial families, the Mortimers, Beauchamps, and Bohuns, although originally of Norman extraction, had through the years jealously
guarded their prerogatives against the encroachment of the
strong Plantagenet Henrys and Edwards, who had gradually in-
creased the power of the throne. These houses were, moreover,
closely allied by marriage and kinship and so shared a great
common interest: the safe-guarding of their fortunes and local
powers from the demands of a king and a court with which they
were fast losing all ties, even those of nationality. And these
families were allied also through common interests and problems
with the great Northern dynasties—the lords of Northumberland,
Gloucester, and Worcester, who were soon to unseat Richard II.

II   *The Alliterative Revival*

In the early years of the fourteenth century this increasing re-
sistance in the North and West not only to the increasing political
strength, but also to the irresponsibility, extravagance, and
foppish elegance of the London court, helped foster the emergence of a school of poetry that revived both the forms and the
essential moral conservatism of pre-invasion England. The poets
of the Alliterative Revival, as this new school is now called, wrote
in the strong accentual verse of the Anglo-Saxons which had apparently never completely died out in Northwest England; and,
though the more sophisticated poets of the school, especially the
Pearl-poet, played on its simple tune an almost endless series of
variations, the basic features of the older verse—the strong four-
stress line, the alliterative bridge over the sharp caesura, the re-
petitive kennings—are always discernible at the heart of the new
stanza forms.

The moral content, what Chaucer typically calls the "sentence,"
of the Alliterative Revival also hearkens back to the heroic age
of English poetry. In poems dealing with Alexander the Great,
William of Palerne, the Trojan War, and the final days of Arthur's
court, the alliterative poets not only reestablished much of the
stern, ringing masculinity of the great Anglo-Saxon and Scandi-
navian epics and battle pieces, but also the forthright morality of
their heroic code of behavior with its emphasis on the close bro-
therhood of leader and thane, the loyalty and devotion of the

individual to the group, and the dignity and heroism of the individual in the face of the hostility of man and nature. And this moral tone is strengthened for the first time in English verse by a heightened social consciousness, by a strong sense of the value of the human spirit, of whatever social class, and by the necessity of justice and fair play in economic life:

> Meakness and mercy, she said, these are the most
> important,
> Have pity on the poor, then please thou our King.[2]

Too much can be made, of course, of this note of social and ecclesiastical reform in Alliterative Revival poetry; we must not credit either North-country poets or barons with having anything resembling a modern liberal zeal for social equality and civil rights. Nowhere, not even in *Piers Plowman,* is there any hint of revolution or of any change in the structure of either Church or society. Langland, in fact, carefully outlines the responsibilities of king, knights, and commoners:

> . . . the nature of a knight or of a king
> Is among their enemies in mortal battles
> To be called and to overcome, in order to defend
> the populace.[3]

But read rightly, it is clear that there is in poems like *Piers Plowman, Wynnere and Wastoure,* and *The Parlement of the Thre Ages* a well-defined note of discontent at the way things are, a protest directed not so much at the system itself, but at its abuses—at the excesses of the royal court, at the degeneration of the clergy and the corruption of doctrine, and at the passing of the decency and order of the old ways:

> All that I gain through wit he wastes through pride;
> I gather, I glean, and he lets it go soon;
> I work and I slave, and he opens the purse.
> Why has this villain no care how men manage affairs?
> His lands all are idle, his tools have been sold,
> Down are his dove-cotes, dry are his pools.[4]

In spite of the restricted viewpoint and technique of this Northern poetry (for not all of these poems exhibit the variety and skill of *Sir Gawain and the Green Knight*), it nevertheless manages at times to manifest in its primitive vigor a far broader and richer range of effects than the elegant poetry written during the same period in London. Chaucer's own early career demonstrates clearly that the concerns of English court poetry in the middle 1300s were still dictated by the late-flowering fashions of a by then decadent French chivalry. The great model and textbook was still the *Roman de la Rose;* and, although Chaucer translated Boethius as well as the *Roman,* the image of the garden of lovers, endlessly refined and varied by Guillaume de Machaut, Froissart, and Eustache Deschamps, dominated the court poetry of London.

III   *Courtly Love*

The principal subject of this poetry was courtly love, or *fin amor,* as it was usually called by its adherents. Although scholars are by no means agreed as to the exact origins of courtly love, it seems reasonably certain that it was of Arabic birth and that it found its way into Provençe in the late eleventh century through erotic poetry brought into southern Europe either by the returning Crusaders or, perhaps, by the Moors. However this new religion of love was imported, it flourished in the South of France. The feudal court of the period was an isolated island of civilization, dominated by its lord and populated almost exclusively by men, "the inferior nobles, the landless knights, the squires, and the pages," [5] none of whom was either free or financially able to marry. Whatever elegance and grace such a court might possess flowed from its lady, who was in every way, socially and culturally, superior to all the men about her, excepting of course her lord.

In this highly artificial society, the new Eastern ideas found an attentive audience. For this poetry, although it celebrated a relationship between the sexes completely at variance with what had hitherto been the accepted norm of Western behavior, was nevertheless neatly fitted to life in the feudal court. No longer was the woman to be regarded as the chattel of her lord or lover, subject to his every whim, deprived of legal rights and of a place of her own in society. The doctrine of courtly love proclaimed her to be what she in fact was in the courts of Provençe: not only the equal of men in intelligence and grace, but their natural master, to whose service they should rightfully dedicate their every effort.

The suitor in this new relationship thus became the servant of his lady and his courtship a series of tests which he had to pass to become worthy of her favor.

To what degree courtly love was actually practiced by the French aristocracy and to what degree it was merely a literary convention of the Provençal poets we shall never know. Either way, however, *fin amor* soon developed into a code, the rules and procedures of which are admirably summarized by Andreas Capellanus, clerk to Eleanor of Aquitaine, one of the most powerful women of her time and one of the great proponents of the new morality. The young lover, who in his youth had scorned love and ridiculed the torments of those in love, is said by Andreas to be awe-struck at first sight of the beloved. Overwhelmed by despair at the hopelessness of his suit, he is plunged into the malady of love, the pains of which deprive him of appetite and sleep. He is rescued from this state through the pity of the lady, who agrees to accept him as one of her servants. On her behalf, he then performs wonderous feats of chivalry, always in hope of winning from her some recognition. Eventually, of course, suitor and lady become more intimately involved, and what had started as adulation and pity becomes adultery. The wedded state of the lady is never a hindrance to the practice of courtly love; it is, in fact, one of its prerequisites: *fin amor,* says Andreas, cannot exist between married partners, who had usually been betrothed at an early age because of political or economic expediency. Thus fidelity and, more especially, secrecy become the greatest of values among courtly lovers, and scandal their most feared enemy.

It is impossible to overstress the impact of courtly love upon Western literature and society. Man in the Classical ages and in the early Middle Ages had frankly regarded woman as his social inferior; the notion that a warrior would devote himself to the service of a woman would have appalled both Achilles and Roland. The greatest Roman treatise on love between the sexes, Ovid's *Ars Amatoria,* is, as C. S. Lewis has pointed out,[6] a satire in which the young man bemused by love is shown to be a fool. Yet Ovid's book was read seriously by medieval courtiers, and his tongue-in-cheek advice to lovers was assiduously followed. Friendship and devotion to one's lord, the great values of the *comitatus* of early chivalry, took a second place to love in the new romances. The principal object of a knight's devotion was no longer his lord or his companion but, paradoxically, his lord's wife.

Such a radical shift in values could hardly fail to create social problems of the greatest magnitude, and indeed the young lover involved in an affair with his lord's wife found himself involved in two irreconcilable conflicts. First, he could not honorably serve both lady and lord, both of whom claimed as their established right his absolute fidelity and devotion. To be untrue to either, even to deceive either, was to break an oath—the vow of a servant of the religion of love or the oath of fealty. Yet the lover, sooner or later, reached the point at which, like Lancelot, he had to choose to whom he would be loyal.

Second, courtly love was from its inception condemned by the Church on two counts—the fact that its end product was adultery rather than marriage, and the fact that it espoused a relationship between the sexes utterly contrary to that of the marital state in which the Church maintained that the husband held undisputed sovereignty and that the sole purpose of sexual union was procreation. Thus courtly love introduced into the very heart of knighthood a tragic contradiction of aims: the young knight was expected to be a devotee of *fin amor,* yet to remain the faithful vassal of his lord; he was inevitably involved in adultery, yet he was expected to serve his God and Church with the utmost fidelity. In time, of course, the dilemmas of chivalry were solved by the sublimation of the practices of courtly love into the routine of normal courtship. Yet the fundamental contradictions are the seeds of the conflicts in Chrétien de Troyes and Sir Thomas Malory and, as we shall see, one of the bases of the testing of Gawain in *Sir Gawain and the Green Knight.*

But if courtly love was responsible for the tragedy of knighthood, it was also the greatest single factor in the creation of *gentilesse,* the code of chivalry. For *fin amor* transformed the military knight, who had been created as a defense against the barbarians and used by the Church as the warlike champion of Christianity, into the courtly gentleman of Chrétien, Malory, and Tennyson. In order to "stonden in his lady grace," the young knight had to acquire the courtly graces. He could no longer rely upon his martial skills to impress her, but was expected to supplement his prowess in arms and hunting with flawless manners and dress and with proficiency in music and poetry. The training of the knight remained basically military in emphasis; but it also came to include the principles of courtly behavior and the practices of humility and courtesy. The new religion of love soon therefore softened and modified the rough standards of earlier knightly conduct.

The new chivalry is nowhere better observed than in the graceful poems of the Provençal troubadours and of the French romancers. In these the knight is seen primarily as courtier and lover, and even his exploits in battle are presented as the natural results of the ennobling effects of love. At its worst, however, courtly-love poetry is stilted, artificial, and totally opposed to the traditional morality of the Church. The poetry of the Alliterative Revival is happily free from the hothouse aromas of the garden of lovers. Not only is the patent immorality of the courtly love situation utterly rejected by the Alliterative Revival poets, but its normal milieu—the decadent, intrigue-ridden chivalric court—is totally foreign to the open, out-of-doors atmosphere of their poetry. We follow Long Will, "wolleward and wete-shoed," through the Malvern Hills and Gawain on his winter journey through the Wirral:

> By a mount on the morn he merrily rides
> To a wood dense and deep that was wondrously wild;
> High hills on each hand, with forests of hoar oaks
> Beneath them most huge, a hundred together.
> Thickly the hazel and hawthorn were tangled,
> Everywhere mantled with moss rough and ragged,
> With many a bird on the bare twigs, mournful,
> That piteously piped for pain of the cold.[7]

It is little wonder that critics such as John Speirs have seen vestiges of early pagan fertility rituals of the contest of winter and summer in these poems;[8] their earthiness and their closeness to the landscapes and weather of the changing seasons make such interpretations, no matter how occasionally strained, inevitable and relevant. And in and through their closeness to the common speech of the land, these poems assume and revive a vitality and a healthy natural morality opposed to the new Continental culture and to the sophisticated courtly view of sex presented, though at the end never really advocated, by Chaucer.

Courtly love appears in Chaucer and in *Sir Gawain and the Green Knight;* but, while in *The Book of the Duchess* and *The Legend of Good Women* it is approved as a way of life and almost as a means of grace, in *Sir Gawain and the Green Knight* it is clearly a temptation and a distraction. Within the courtly frame seduction may well be an experience to be dealt with politely and with a great deal of tact and charm; but it is, as Gawain finally discovers, a mortal danger both to the individual and to his society.

IV *The Poet*

The *Pearl*-poet then is of the Alliterative Revival, though it is of course doubtful that he ever thought of himself as being a member of any school. We do not in fact know his actual name or station in life, although scholars have attempted to identify him with known figures of the time. One scholar has proposed, for example, that he was a clerk[9] in the household of Enguerrand de Coucy, Earl of Bedford, who himself is thought by the same scholar to be the model for the Green Knight.[10] He has been identified as one Huchown of the Awle Ryall, to whom at various times have been attributed most of the unidentified poems of the late fourteenth century.[11]

Working directly from internal evidence in *Pearl* that the poet is perhaps elegizing the death of a child named Margaret or Margery, two noted students of the period have proposed that the poet was a clerk in the household of the Earl of Pembroke, whose daughter Margaret died in 1369.[12] These scholars have even suggested that either of two such clerks, John Donne and John Prat, might well be the *Pearl*-poet. Again, on the basis of the books read by the poet, one commentator has proposed one John of Erghome, a North-country Oxford scholar whose library might well resemble that of the poet.[13] The *Pearl*-poet, on the basis of the geography described in *Sir Gawain and the Green Knight,* has been assigned a place in the household of the great John of Gaunt.[14] And perhaps the most famous, as well as the most opinionated, student of the poems has suggested the Ralph Strode whom Chaucer refers to in *Troilus and Criseyde* as "philosophical Strode." [15] There is no lack of claimants for the honor of being the fourteenth century's second poet.

No applicant for the honor, however, has ever been acceptable to the whole fraternity of those students who have seriously dealt with the problem. Nor is it important that one should, for the poems themselves reveal clearly enough the sort of man that wrote them. His interests and opinions, his background and training, and even something of his personality and character are revealed through these four poems, which are for the Middle Ages exceedingly intimate documents. Though it is of little consequence to our understanding of the poems as such, the personality of the *Pearl*-poet is much more clearly evident in his writings than is that of Shakespeare, the facts of whose life are well known, yet who speaks always through the mouths of his characters.

It is evident, for example, that the *Pearl*-poet was for his age an extremely well-read man, particularly in contemporary literature. His works evince his familiarity not only with St. Jerome's great Vulgate text of the Bible, with which he shows what may well be a professional clerk's knowledge, but also with the standard scriptural commentaries of the Church Fathers. He had also read and was obviously influenced by *The Consolation of Philosophy*, Boethius' work concerning the role that fortune and chance play in the lives of men. His vocabulary and images show traces of his having read the *Roman de la Rose*, *The Divine Comedy*, *The Aeneid*, the Old French version of Mandeville's *Travels*, Boccaccio's elegy, *Olympia*, and perhaps part of *The Canterbury Tales*.[16]

The *Pearl*-poet's use of the concepts of theology and of Bible stories as basic themes in *Pearl*, *Patience*, and *Purity* reveals that he was in all probability a clerk, though he was not necessarily attached to the house of Enguerrand de Coucy or of the Earl of Pembroke or of any other known nobleman. From the sharpness of his awareness of the multi-sided theological issues of his time, it is possible that he was educated in the monastic schools or perhaps even in the university.[17] He may even have been, late in life, a monk.[18] One scholar, as a matter of fact, maintains that the central theological discussion of *Pearl*, the long debate between the dreamer and the child concerning the relative weight of grace and good works in the process of salvation, demonstrates that the poet was a highly original and perhaps heretical theologian and that in his views he is a forerunner of the Reformation in England.[19]

There is some evidence also that he was more than usually ac-

quainted with the details of courtly life. There are distinct echoes
in his works of legal phraseology[20] and, interestingly enough, of
the language of the apothecary.[21] He obviously had a thorough
grounding in the various sorts of medieval music.[22] His knowledge of hunting, of heraldry, and of the arming of knights,[23] as
manifested in *Sir Gawain and the Green Knight,* reveals an intimate familiarity with court life, a fact that would seem to negate
the possibility of his having taken monastic orders at an early age.

Certain suppositions may also be made about the kind of
countryside with which he was familiar. He was almost certainly
a country man by birth and by inclination. As Savage says, he is
"completely lacking in the 'commercial atmosphere' that one
sometimes savors" in Chaucer.[24] The imagery of his poems
abounds with pictures of natural landscapes very like the hilly,
almost mountainous, regions of Lancashire, Staffordshire, and
Cheshire. He is most at home with mountains and running
streams:

> In the midst of a glade a mound, as it might be,
> A smooth, swelling knoll by the side of the water,
> The falls of a rivulet running close by;
> In its banks the brook bubbled as though it were boiling,[25]

and with the wild flowers of the North:

> Upon the mound where my pearl fell,
> Tall, shadowing herbs grew bright and sheen,
> Gilliflower, ginger and gromwell,
> With peonies powdered all between.[26]

One, however, is tempted to go far beyond these hints of personality and to read in, or rather into, these poems the poet's own
history of personal tragedy. A number of the early critics, dis-
regarding the fact that all the internal stylistic evidence points to
an arrangement of the poems in which *Patience* and *Purity* clearly
precede *Pearl* and *Sir Gawain and the Green Knight,* saw *Pearl*
as the first movement of a great mental struggle occasioned by
the poet's loss of his two year old daughter.[27] *Pearl* became for
them the poet's tortured expression of a grief so great that it
caused him to doubt the goodness of God, to abandon the courtly
interests of happier days during which he had written *Sir Gawain*

and the Green Knight, to plunge himself into the religious life, and to express in *Purity* and, more emphatically, in *Patience* the consolation he discovered there. And certainly no reader will for a moment doubt that the poems reveal their author to be a man of great compassion and well acquainted with grief.

But, while such a theory is tempting—not only because it provides a unifying device by which the poems may be linked thematically, but also because it settles forever the problem of unity of authorship—this view of the poems is simply untenable in the light of the development of poetic talent revealed in the poems themselves. *Patience* and *Purity* are purely alliterative; and, while they demonstrate in structure, meter, and imagery the signs of unmistakable genius, they cannot match the brilliant subtleties, particularly in meter, that grace *Pearl* and *Sir Gawain and the Green Knight.* So, however great the temptation to read *Patience* and *Pearl* as the protestations of a grief-stricken father, it is far wiser to see them as genre poems demonstrating the poet's increasing ability to work within the conventional poetic types of his age and his increasing awareness of the effects to be gained by mixing English and French verse forms. All the evidence, therefore—metrical, stylistic, and thematic—would seem to point to the arrangement: *Patience, Purity, Pearl, Sir Gawain and the Green Knight.*[28]

V *Unity of Authorship*

It will be noted that everything I have said about the *Pearl*-poet is based on the assumption that the four poems of Cotton Nero A.x. were written by the same man; and indeed there seems little reason to doubt that this is the case. Only one modern scholar, as a matter of fact, has challenged seriously this generally accepted unity of authorship,[29] and even his carefully framed arguments have found little acceptance. The poems are without doubt written in precisely the same north-west Midland dialect and share in common not only a number of strongly localized north-west Midland vocabulary items not found in other poems of the Alliterative Revival, but more strikingly a number of highly individualistic word forms which cannot be accounted for on the basis of literary convention and imitation. There are evident in the four poems a number of common stylistic devices, notably the repetition of "framing" lines at the beginning and

end of all four poems, the device of frequently calling an audience
to attention, and the occasional apology of the poet for his inability to describe properly some overwhelming experience.[30]
Certain unique habits of phraseology seem also to demonstrate
common authorship, particularly the paraphrasing of "God" and
"Lord" by means of relative clauses and the use of "and." [31] Fur-
thermore, as Robert Menner points out, the very absence in
Cotton Nero A.x. of repetitions of favorite half-lines, a device
common among cruder poets, is itself an indication of unity of
authorship.[32]

The poems also reveal a number of verbal parallels. There is a
rather unusual praising of the pearl as a symbol of chastity, for
example, in both *Pearl* and *Purity;* repeated mention of the beati-
fic vision in *Patience, Purity,* and *Pearl;*[33] and such a great number of similar passages, particularly between *Purity* and *Sir Gawain and the Green Knight,* that Menner is moved to claim for
them "indubitable proof of common authorship." [34] There is evident in all four poems, moreover, a fondness for describing the
same kinds of out-of-doors scenes, a fact that indicates not only a
love of the woods and streams of the North, but common authorship of the poems.

Most striking of all, however, is the poet's concern in all four
poems with morality, particularly with the virtue of chastity, and
with the value of humility and patience as aids in accepting the
trials that life is sure to bring. Throughout the poems of Cotton
Nero A.x. one is conscious of a wholly unified and individual
point of view and of the presence of an author whose central
concern is with the trials of life—with the death of children and
the seemingly impossible tasks that God sends his own, with the
degenerative effects of luxury, and with the insinuating temptations of chivalry. As one critic has suggested, "in *Purity* and
Patience the author seems to be working out with great care the
moral values of these virtues in human life, and in *Pearl* and *Sir
Gawain* he seems to be putting his conclusions to the test." [35]

And everywhere this unknown genius espouses the same answer—the humble acceptance of God's will—to the grief and suffering he knows to be inevitable in a fallen world: "When heavy
hearts are hurt with contempt or other ills / Forbearance may
comfort them and lighten the blow. . . ." [36] Or again, he writes:

> To the Prince's will had my heart bent,
> And sought but what to me was given,
> Held fast to that, with true intent,
> As my Pearl prayed me out of heaven;
> Did I to God my thoughts present,
> More in His mysteries had I thriven.[37]

Certainly one need not accept the biographical fallacies of the early critics to sense in all four poems the presence of a single author whose works, whatever their immediate intentions, bear witness to their creator's suffering and meditation.

VI *The Dates and Place of the Poems*

There are many problems also involved in dating the poems. The manuscript itself, judging from the scribal handwriting, was copied not later than 1400. The individual poems, however, are very difficult to date, especially since their relative chronology is by no means certain. *Pearl* seems to have been written after 1360, the date of Boccaccio's *Olympia,* one of its sources.[38] *Sir Gawain and the Green Knight* was composed almost certainly after 1345, the probable date of the founding of the Order of the Garter, the motto of which—*Hony Soyt Qui Mal Pence* ("Shame be to him who thinks evil")—concludes the poem, and the details of costume and architecture would place it even later, in the last quarter of the century.[39] If the poet used, as he almost certainly did, the French version of Mandeville's *Travels* as one of the sources of *Purity,* then this poem must have been written after 1356, the probable date of publication of Mandeville's book.[40] And since the B-text of *Piers Plowman* apparently echoes *Patience,* a date before 1377 would seem feasible for that poem.[41]

Since, however, *Patience* and *Purity* almost certainly precede *Pearl* and *Sir Gawain,* it is difficult to assign the author anything resembling a clearly fixed period of artistic flowering, although the period 1360–1390 would seem to satisfy nearly everyone. Whatever the dates assigned, however, the conclusion to be drawn would seem to be that the *Pearl*-poet developed his techniques and themes over a number of years, a fact that would place him, like Chaucer and unlike Gower, in that category of poets with whom poetry is an avocation rather than an occupation. Four poems in thirty years is clearly a small output for a man of such genius. Yet the poems evidence such a range of theme and technique and such a steady progress in the subtleties of meter and expression that it does not seem overly conjectural to assume that the *Pearl*-poet was a slow, careful craftsman building solidly and slowly his great structures of poetry.

Like the dates of the poems, their geographical origins present an unusual number of problems. The general area assigned to the poet, mainly on the basis of dialect—and there is little chance of scribal influence on the dialect—is that of the northwest Midlands, with Lancashire and Cheshire the strongest possibilities.[42] Only a few scholars, who have dissented from the prevailing opinion, have named Yorkshire and Derbyshire[43] as alternative areas. The evidence of local knowledge and place names, particularly in *Sir Gawain and the Green Knight*, points to a close familiarity with the countryside of Northern Wales and with the Wirral, a dense forest, apparently a haunt of bandits, in northwest Cheshire.[44] As with the problem of date, however, the actual placing of the poet is less important than the general conclusion to be drawn from the evidence: that his heart would seem to lie in the mountains, far removed from the commercial and political bustle of the great city.

This discussion has attempted to touch upon problems connected with the four poems of the *Pearl*-poet which very likely will never be solved to the satisfaction of everyone. But as to the literary values of the poems themselves there has never been any dissension; *Pearl, Purity, Patience*, and *Sir Gawain and the Green Knight*, different as they are in genre and tone, are universally acclaimed masterpieces of the English literary tradition. Their merit and their value to the reader, moreover, are of those rare types that increase with familiarity; the more one inspects their techniques and structures, the more they captivate. The ensuing chapters attempt to illuminate as many aspects of these remarkable poems as possible—not to "dissect," as another Northern poet put it, but to expose their many charms and wonders.

CHAPTER 2

Pearl

THE poem Richard Morris called *Pearl*[1] is the first of the four poems of Cotton Nero A.x., and whatever its rightful place in the chronology of the poet's works may be,[2] it makes an excellent point of departure for a study of the *Pearl*-poet.

I *The Dream-Vision*

The poem is of a type common in the late Middle Ages—the dream-vision in which a dreamer, who is also the "I" narrator of the poem, falls asleep and experiences in a dream a series of events which are, as a rule, both fantastic and allegorical. It is a kind of literature no longer popular, but it functioned in its own time as a form of expression that could present an experience that was clearly a fiction—the dream itself—under a superficial guise of credibility—the authority of the known and identifiable author-narrator-dreamer. The mechanics of the dream-vision thus provided for the medieval reader a means by which he could suspend at least temporarily his distrust of the purely fictional and could accept the fantastic images of the dream-fiction for the moment as having the authority of truth.

The need for such a technique seems to us modern readers totally unnecessary. We are perfectly accustomed to make the mental adjustment required to accept without question as "truth" what Henry James called a writer's "given," the basic fiction—a demoniac whaling ship, or a land of little people, or even the England of 1984—that underlies any piece of literature, the immediate and unquestioning acceptance of which is necessary to our continuing to read the work.

Medieval readers, however, with their ingrained belief in authority and tradition and with their distrust of originality could not easily adopt such an attitude. Just as they demanded an "authority" for their chronicles of the past (even though that author-

35

ity might be wholly fictional), so they demanded for even the
most obviously made-up accounts of visions and dreams an
eyewitness, a real and identifiable narrator in whom they could
place their credence.

The dream-vision thus became an ideal framework for allegory
since here the most obviously allegorical personifications could
be presented under a form of fantasy—the dream—completely
familiar and hence credible to the reader. Every man had to some
degree felt in his own dreams the stunned awe with which the
dreamer in *Pearl* or *The Book of the Duchess* or *Piers Plowman*
first perceives the strange landscape of the dream world. And
every man had sensed also that just behind the fantastic and un-
familiar shapes of his own dreams lay some revelation of truth.
The majority of medieval people still felt strongly that the ex-
terior forms of nature spoke to them constantly, presenting them
with heavenly truths and lessons, but that, since the Fall, these
forms spoke only in the mysterious language of symbols. The
lion cub sleeping for the three days immediately following its
birth thus illuminated in some strange way the crucified Christ,
and the snake shedding its skin in the new spring enjoined men
to put away their old sins and to be born again in their risen
Lord. Thus men felt that in the same way their dreams sometimes
revealed to them truths beyond the grasp of their waking in-
telligences.

This peculiar mixture of personal poet-narrator and allegorical
subject matter is responsible for the most perplexing of the purely
literary problems involved in *Pearl*: whether the poem is in
fact an elegy on the death of the poet-narrator's two year old
daughter or whether it is, or even could be, purely allegorical,
with the death of the child having no referent in the life of the
poet-narrator and thus functioning only as a literary device. This
question, of course, involves not only *Pearl* itself, but all the
dream-vision poems of the age and leads directly to a major point
in the study of literary history: was any writer, regardless of
skill, at this point in the development of fiction capable of creating a purely objective persona, an "I" narrator completely di-
vorced from himself, existing only in his imagination and dwelling
only within the confines of his fiction? Literary historians, who as
a rule tend to see all literature in terms of literary conventions

and influences, usually judge such a creation impossible, but the poets themselves often seem to be unaware that their own literary works are wholly bound by the literature of the past and so often manage to escape from the conventions of their own times to speak directly to our condition.

II *The Action*

Pearl opens with a situation common in this kind of literature; the author-narrator-dreamer is discovered alone in a lovely garden where, he tells us, he recently lost "through grass to earth" a pearl that had no peer: "So round, so radiant to mine eyes, / So smooth she seemed, so small to hold. . . ."[3] In agony he has visited the garden to grieve at the mound where "into dark molds" the pearl disappeared, and he has come this day in "August in a high season" to mourn anew this loss.

Soon, however, he falls into an exhausted sleep and his spirit "through God's grace" travels to a marvelously beautiful forest and meadow:

> In beauty shone each fair hillside
> With crystal cliffs in shining row,
> While bright woods everywhere abide,
> Their boles as blue as indigo;
> Like silver clear the leaves spread wide,
> That on each spray quick-quivering grow;
> If a flash of light across them glide
> With shimmering sheen they gleam and glow. . . .   (73–80)

Here he miraculously discovers a kind of peace, and he forgets for a moment his grief. Then he suddenly finds himself on the bank of a stream, itself more marvelous than the meadow:

> The beauties of that stream were steep,
> All radiant banks of beryl bright;
> Sweet-sighing did the water sweep,
> With murmuring music running light;
> Within its bed fair stones lay deep;
> As if through glass they glowed, as white
> As streaming stars when tired men sleep
> Shine in the sky on a winter night.   (109–16)

Along the banks of the stream, moreover, he experiences not only
an end to sorrow, but more positively a great bliss and an increasing joy:

> There was more of marvel and of grace
> Than I could tell, howe'er I tried;
> The human heart that could embrace
> A tenth part were well satisfied. . . .   (133–36)

But try as he may, he cannot cross the miraculous stream to the
paradise beyond.

Suddenly he sees standing beyond the stream a maiden, the
"precious one in pearls bedight" (192). To his first stunned in-
quiries, she replies that she is indeed the lost pearl, and that she
has escaped the prison of nature to find eternal life in Paradise,
where he cannot living join her. The narrator's response to her
explanations is interesting: he is more concerned with his own
grief than with her happiness, and she is quick, almost rude, in
revealing to him the selfishness of his concern:

> 'Twere better thou thy fate shouldst bless,
> And love thy God, through weal and woe;
> For anger wins not happiness;
> Who must, shall bear; bend thy pride low. . . .   (341–44)

He apologizes immediately; and she, forgiving him his "master-
ful mood and haughty pride" (401), offers to tell him something
of her life. But at her first statement, that she lives as a queen in
Heaven, the narrator again objects, saying that surely she must be
mistaken, that at her death she knew "no Paternoster . . . nor
creed" (485), and that God would surely not go so far astray from
the ideals of justice as to so honor a mere babe.

At this point the two argue for a time the relative merits of
grace and good works in achieving salvation. The pearl-maiden
recounts at length the parable of the workers in the vineyard and
maintains that her place in Heaven is hers not by right, but entirely through the grace of God:

> More gladness have I, herewithin,
> Of flower of life, and noble name,

> Than all men in the world might win,
> Who thought their righteous deeds to name.   (577–80)

The narrator, on the other hand, maintains that, since the Scriptures affirm that God "requitest each for his deed's sake" (595), the maiden's place as queen is undeserved; and the child answers by again asserting that the "grace of God is great enow" (612) not only to compensate for all earth's injustices, known and unknown, but also to overcome all mortal notions of what is in fact just and unjust. She then explains the special glory of the innocent in Heaven, a situation that, again, the narrator cannot accept.

At last, having told him of the suffering of Christ on earth, the pearl-maiden shows the narrator a vision of the apocalyptic New Jerusalem and herself among the other innocents in the retinue of Christ. In a joyous effort to join the maiden, the dreamer attempts to plunge into the stream that separates them and is sharply awakened from his dream. The poem closes with the poet's statement that he is reconciled to the loss of the pearl, having been assured of her place in Heaven and of the goodness of the God who placed her there.

III   *The Persona*

Even such a cursory summary as this should reveal the structural problem presented by the point of view from which the poem is presented. We are confronted, on the one hand, with certain obvious personal references: the maiden herself refers to her having left the "world's woe" (761) at a "young and tender" age (412); the dreamer asserts that at her death she was not yet two years old and that she had learned neither Paternoster nor Creed (483–485); upon first seeing her, the dreamer recognizes her immediately (164) and asserts that she was "nearer than aunt or niece" to him (233). The conclusion that the poem revolves about the death of a child and that it is thus, on the literary level, an elegy is almost unavoidable.

But does the poem revolve about an *actual* death? Is the poet bemoaning the death of an *actual* two year old, his daughter or another child "nearer than aunt or niece" to him? And here we are thrown back again upon what little we can ascertain about the literary practices of medieval poets. As we have said, the medieval poet felt it necessary to present even his most obvious fictions as though they were actual happenings. In medieval literature we are thus presented either with the sort of historical objectivity noticeable in heroic works like *The Song of Roland* and the *Njalssaga* that indeed do have a known basis in history or with a story told by a narrator, like any of Chrètien's romances, that substitutes the authority of the narrator for the known historical background of the epic.

And quite often it is apparent that, in order to lend credibility to his tale, the author has identified himself closely with the narrator of his fiction, even to the extent of crediting to the narrator, again as a means of gaining authority for his works, the external facts of his own life. In the very first romances, for example, Chrétien identifies himself with his "I" narrator by stating, as narrator in *Lancelot* and in *Perceval,* that he, as author, received his subject matter from his noble patrons. In *The Divine Comedy,* Dante the Pilgrim begins the poem with an allusion to Dante the Writer's age in 1300, the dramatic date of the poem, and so clearly demonstrates his intention to identify Writer and Pilgrim; and in *Piers Plowman,* Long Will the Dreamer and William Langland the Writer are identified by means of the facts of biography common to both.

That such a convention existed is therefore certain, but there are observable and severe differences in the extent to which poet and narrator were in fact identified in medieval literature. It seems clear, for example, that at least in rare instances medieval writers were capable of creating totally independent personae, first-person narrators who were purely fictional and whose identity bore no relationship in either life facts or personality to those of their creators. The Sir John Mandeville who narrates the famous *Travels* almost certainly never existed and the book as we have it is anonymous.

More importantly, however, there are differences even in those works in which writer and narrator are superficially identified in name or in biography in the degree to which the *character* and *personality* of the persona mirror those of the writer. In the course of an enlightening discussion of the use of the persona in the poems of William Butler Yeats, T. S. Eliot, and Ezra Pound, George T. Wright has asserted that in the creation of a persona, any poet, no matter of what period, is of necessity, whether consciously or unconsciously, highly selective in his choice of those

characteristics of his personality he exposes to the public view.[4]
Thus any persona must to some degree be separable from its creator; existing only within the boundaries of his creation, it is defined by its own particular speech and actions there.

Apparently such a truth was recognized by the earliest writers.
In distinguishing between simple narration and imitation, Plato
attempts to define the possible "voices" or points of view that
poets, notably Homer, had used long before his own time.[5] And
Aristotle in further limiting the use of "voice" in imitation makes it
clear that an author may without difficulty assume, for the purpose of "imitating" life, which to Aristotle involved a high degree
of selection and concentration, the point of view of a character
who is essentially an extension of himself.[6]

The problem of the persona in medieval literature is thus basically one of degree. Chaucer, to use the clearest example, certainly never intended his audience, who after all knew him intimately, to identify the personal characteristics of the narrator in
The Book of the Duchess with those of its author.[7] The narrator's
statement that he is ignorant of Classical mythology and his ap-
palling density in failing to recognize the source of the Black
Knight's grief are clearly parts of a dramatic fiction, deliberately
created in order to present a rather slow-witted persona on whom
the facts of the Black Knight's situation will be lost. Thus by
means of a dramatic irony within the poem we always know more
than does Chaucer the Narrator about the situation at hand,
though less of course than does Chaucer the Writer, who not
only created the entire fiction, but arranged for the reader's role
in it.

The same point can certainly be made about the lazy "Geoffrey"
of *The House of Fame*; about the overly-sympathetic and senti-
mental narrator of *Troilus and Criseyde*, who is half in love with
Criseyde himself; and about the cheerful, naïve Chaucer the Pilgrim of *The Canterbury Tales* who, among other things, gives us
all the clues necessary for us to guess that Oswald the Reeve is
actually the old carpenter of "The Miller's Tale," but who never
reveals that he sees the point himself. Indeed, a clear separation
of Chaucer the Pilgrim and Chaucer the Writer would seem the
basic component of any serious reading of *The Canterbury Tales*
as a dynamic and unified poem.

Chaucer's use of himself as a distinct persona in his own poetry is only the most obvious example of what would seem to be a rather common practice among the greatest medieval authors. For example, Francis Fergusson has compared Dante's use of himself as Pilgrim to the use made by Henry James of a "central intelligence," "visible himself as a particular individual, yet revealing to the reader both the story and its meaning as he learns it." [8] Thus Dante the Writer, "when he reminds us of his existence, is outside the fictive world of the poem; the Pilgrim is the protagonist of the drama, the center of each scene." [9]

Needless to say, there are critics who do not allow for this separation of author and persona, but who feel that the identification of creator and creature is one that we are "*bound* to make": "For if we turn to the dreams and allegories of Langland's age, we find the dreamer insisting on his personality, mentioning his name, or being called by his name: and the name and person of the dreamer are never those of an imaginary figure—they are always the name and person of the poet." [10]

The author of this statement ignores a distinction basic to the study of the literature of any age: the poet may lend to his persona his own name and some of the facts of his life in order to inspire credence and to lend authority to his work, especially if he lives in an age that demands such aids to credibility; but he is certainly free within the bounds of that work to create whatever characterizations, including that of himself, best fit his *dramatic* purposes. The "I" of *The Canterbury Tales* is no more Geoffrey Chaucer than the "I" 's of *As I Lay Dying* are William Faulkner.

Moreover, any piece of literature which involves an "I" narrator must by definition be dramatic; it must involve character development, rather than simply character presentation. We identify ourselves, unconsciously and immediately, with the "I" of any given tale, and we accompany him, willy-nilly, on his journey. We see only as he sees; we learn only what he learns; but we do see and we do learn. And of all the forms which literature may take, the dream-vision of the Middle Ages would seem the genre in which some degree of dramatic development is not only expected, but implicitly required. For it is the nature of allegory to *dramatize,* to give a local habitation and a name to an internal struggle for decision, to a progression of thought.

In the *Roman de la Rose*, we move from uncertainty and doubt to joyful triumph, in *The Book of the Duchess* from confusion to understanding, and in *Piers Plowman* from the first gropings for salvation to the final glorification of Man in Christ. And even in the most typical and hence most stereotyped of the dream-visions, in the repeated quest of the knight into the Other World of the Celtic fairyland, the development of a man's understanding of life can be seen to underlie the type, if not always the particular example of it. It is indeed contrary to the whole nature of the genre to have a dream-vision allegory which does not involve, as E. V. Gordon has said, "a real process of thought culminating in some resolution or turning-point of the interior life." [11]

It has been some time since I wrote the word "pearl." Yet the preceding discussion is perhaps the key, or at least one of the keys, to what is essential to an understanding of the poem—of the fact that the poem, as the poet has left it to us, may very well be *both* a fact of actual life and a vision, an elegy for a real child who becomes within the poem an allegorical, or better a symbolic, figure representing one or perhaps a number of concepts. Once the possibility of this point of view towards the poem is granted, the arguments that have raged over the "meaning" of the pearl-maiden can be seen as advancing complementary rather than opposing interpretations, and all of the interpretations may be assessed in relation to the dramatic heart of the poem, the movement of the narrator from grief and confusion to consolation and understanding.

III *Allegory*

Richard Morris, who prepared the first printed edition of *Pearl* for the Early English Text Society in 1864, saw the poem as an elegy on the death of the poet's daughter, an interpretation supported, as we have seen, by a number of allusions within the poem.[12] The elegiac reading was first seriously challenged forty years later by W. H. Schofield, who maintained in two lengthy articles that the child was simply a figment of the poet's imagination, inspired by his reading of Boccaccio's "Fourteenth Eclogue," the so-called *Olympia,* which elegizes the death of a small child who appears to her father glorified in a vision.[13] *Pearl,* declared Schofield, was thus essentially allegorical, though not systematically so, and didactic in nature, since the child represents purity, or "clean maidenhood," in exactly the same fashion that the figures of the *Roman de la Rose* represent Fear or Shame or Pity.

Schofield's view was immediately challenged, most sharply by G. G. Coulton.[14] But his major point, the allegorical nature of the poem, once established, held on; and a variety of opinions as to the exact significance of the allegory have since been advanced— that the child symbolizes the Holy Eucharist, through which by grace Man may establish union with God;[15] that she represents, in a curious mixture of allegory and elegy, the lost innocence of the narrator as well as his lost innocent, the child;[16] that she is the "lost sweetness of God" for which the poet now mourns in a state of "spiritual dryness," the interior desolation of the spirit;[17] that she is a non-allegorical literary device used simply to present a lesson in divine grace;[18] that she is the beauty of the immortal soul [19] and of the Kingdom of Heaven;[20] that she is the potentially perfect soul;[21] that she is the soul of Man made regenerate by baptism and by God's favor.[22] And these are only a few of the major allegorical interpretations of the poem. When we examine the comments on individual passages and even lines, it becomes evident that the poem has been done almost to death by its interpreters.

This tendency, initiated sixty years ago, to see the poem purely as allegory has perhaps reached its natural culmination in the work of those recent critics who specialize in applying the known canons of exegetical criticism to *Pearl*. In working with *Pearl* two of these critics have used as a point of departure St. Thomas Aquinas' famous statement in the *Summa Theologica*—later applied by both Dante and Boccaccio, among others, to secular literature—of the possible levels of meaning at which a passage of Scripture might be read:

The author of Holy Writ is God, in whose power it is to signify His meaning, not by words only (as man also can do), but also by things themselves. So, whereas in every other science things are signified by words, this science has the property, that the things signified by the words have themselves also a signification. Therefore that first significa- tion whereby words signify things belongs to the first sense, the histori- cal or literal. That signification whereby things signified by words have themselves also a signification is called the spiritual sense, which is based on the literal, and presupposes it. Now this spiritual sense has a threefold division. For as the Apostle says (Heb. x., I) the Old Law is a figure of the New Law, and Dionysius says (Coel. Hier I.) *the New Law itself is a figure of future glory*. Again, in the New Law, whatever our Head has done is a type of what we ought to do. Therefore, so far as the things of the Old Law signify the things of the New Law, there is the allegorical sense; so far as the things done in Christ, or so far as the things which signify Christ, are types of what we ought to do, there is the moral sense. But so far as they signify what relates to eternal glory, there is the anagogical sense. Since the literal sense is that which the author intends, and since the author of Holy Writ is God, Who by one act comprehends all things by His intellect, it is not unfitting, as Augustine says (Confess. xii), if, even according to the literal sense, one word in Holy Writ should have several senses.[23]

Thus one critic, viewing the poem as an allegory of the place of innocence in the scheme of things, maintains that on the literal level, the pearl is simply a jewel; on the allegorical, an innocent young girl; on the tropological, the means by which the soul through penance gains innocency; and on the anagogical, the life of innocence itself in the New Jerusalem.[24] Another critic, working out of a slightly different interpretation of St. Thomas' categories, sees the child, literally and historically, as an unresolved question of identification; allegorically, as the loss of spiritual peace; morally, as the loss of faith; and, anagogically, as the loss of Heaven itself.[25] To this critic the theme of the poem is the loss of innocence at all levels through the loss of the pearl, which is itself allegorically all those things which are lost.

The poem, in its various allegorical interpretations, has thus come to mean, if not all things to all men, then at least a great many things to a great many men. And through the use of the multi-leveled scheme of interpretation laid down by St. Thomas and advocated by a number of modern critics as a key to the understanding of all medieval literature, the possibilities for allegorical interpretation have been multiplied almost endlessly.[26] No one would challenge, I think, the relevance of Thomas' argument to the interpretation of Scripture; Holy Writ is by definition inspired by God and written for our benefit and so is open by its very nature to a wide range of readings at a number of levels, though not perhaps always in quite as mechanical a fashion as Thomas and the other Scholiasts, in their usual orderly way, envisioned it.

The moot point is, of course, the application of the theory to secular literature; for, while a great number of theologians advocate in their writings this sort of systematic exegesis, very few poets do. Thus, while I agree with Robert Kaske, the most flexible,

I think, of the exegetical critics, that there is "some strong indirect evidence" [27] for the presence among medieval secular writers of a large body of exegetical lore, I do not therefore believe that any medieval poet—including, in spite of his own statement, Dante in the "Paradiso" [28]—was able to construct a poem that operated consistently and equally validly on the four levels laid down by the Schoolmen for the interpretation of Scripture.

In a sense, this lack of coherence and consistency marks all of the allegorical interpretations of *Pearl*. For above all other literary qualities, allegory demands consistency. The *Roman de la Rose* and *Pilgrim's Progress* are capable of being read throughout their lengths at two distinct levels of meaning, and two levels of meaning are about all the mind can either conceive of or control simultaneously. While it is thus clear, as E. V. Gordon says, that there are "minor allegories within *Pearl*," [29] the parable of the vineyard being the best example, and that the poem is filled with symbols, notably the pearl itself, it seems equally certain that no critic has framed an allegorical interpretation that will function constantly and consistently throughout the poem.

IV *Symbolism, Theology, and Imagery*

A number of critics have therefore simply abandoned both the elegiac and the allegorical approaches to the whole poem in order to stress the symbolism and the imagery of its parts.[30] Indeed, the poem is filled with individual images and with image clusters of all kinds—of flowers and growing things and of the harvest, of blood and water, of light, of music and jewels, and of the Cities of God and Man—all of which essentially point, as Fr. Edwin Cuffe states, to "the bounty of God" and "the overwhelming extravagance with which God rewards his good servants" [31] and to the vast difference in the poem between heavenly and earthly values; as a result, the imagery promotes the moral purpose of the poem.

Of all the symbols with which the poem deals, however, the most prominent and the most immediately effective is that of the pearl itself.[32] Just as the medieval bestiaries interpreted allegorically the characteristics of animals, medieval lapidaries interpreted the symbolic qualities of gems; and in these books the pearl, or *margarita,* is continually cited as a symbol of purity, presumably of course because of its whiteness.[33] As such, it was often associated with virginity and with the Blessed Virgin herself, and so came in time to form the basis of a cult which drew its membership from the ranks of courtly maidens and which took as its patron the third-century St. Margaret of Antioch.

Thus the whole symbolic tradition of the pearl comes to bear upon the poem; the pearl is here both the maiden, who might well have been named Margery or Margarita, and the symbol of her spotless body and soul. She is arrayed in pearls: she wears upon her breast the "pearl of great price" and upon her head a crown of pearls. At the height of her argument, she enjoins the dreamer to renounce the foolish world and to search for his own spotless pearl. In this way, the symbol of the pearl, imbued with all the connotative symbolic richness of its centuries of development, dominates the symbolism of the poem and enriches our perception of the place of the innocent in the hierarchy of Heaven.

Other students have found a key to the meaning of the poem precisely in this question of hierarchy and in the long theological debate between narrator and maiden centering on the Church's view of salvation. Nor can anyone doubt that the illumination of doctrine is one of the poet's purposes; in fact, it is impossible to come to grips with the poem without some understanding both of the doctrine argued and of the intensity of the argument. Certainly the great issues of theology, like the one of the relative weight of grace and merit in the scheme of salvation, were far more alive in the Middle Ages than they are today. Scholar, priest, plowman, knight, and merchant all lived closely within the Church's sphere of influence; their problems were her problems and her debates theirs. Thus, medieval literature is filled with debate on theological issues—the virtuous pagan in *St. Erkenwald,* free will and predestination in "The Nun's Priest's Tale," and the whole gamut of contemporary religious problems in *Piers Plowman.* And surprisingly the range of opinion was extensive; medieval theology was by no means a settled affair, and one has only to examine the writings of the Church Fathers to see the amount of pure speculation indulged in by the Schoolmen themselves.

The orthodoxy of the *Pearl*-poet's theology in the debate between maiden and dreamer went unquestioned until 1904, when an important article by Carleton F. Brown presented the poet as a learned ecclesiastic whose theological opinions in the poem were clearly in opposition to the accepted doctrines of his time.[34] The pearl-maiden's insistence in the poem that the "grace of God is

great enough" for salvation and that there is equality among the
saved in Heaven is, according to Brown, in marked contradiction
to the system of rewards for good deeds established by SS. Jerome, Augustine, and Gregory. The poem thus disregards patristic
authority and tradition, relying instead on Scripture and making
salvation purely a matter of grace uninfluenced by merit. In
Brown's view, the *Pearl*-poet is a forerunner of the sixteenth-
century Protestant Reformation since he maintains, as does
Luther, that salvation is by grace alone. But, although Brown's
views did much to focus the attention of readers on the theology
of the poem, few, if any, scholars have agreed with his conclusions
or followed his lead.

Much of the confusion surrounding the theology of the poem is
dispelled where it is recalled and kept always in the foreground of
any interpretation that the maiden's arguments are part of a dramatic situation within the poem. She is presented by the poet as
arguing actively and at times vehemently with the narrator in an
attempt to break through his stubborn earthliness and to force
him to recognize the truth of the vision which he has been permitted to see. Thus it is natural that she should to some degree
overstate her case and overemphasize in her eagerness certain aspects of the doctrines she is advocating.

Although, as Brown shows, she repeatedly emphasizes the
place of grace in the process of salvation and the equality of reward in Heaven, she is not therefore heretical in her views.[35] The
Fathers had agreed—though they differed of course slightly
among themselves—that the sacrament of baptism itself conferred
saving grace, as the maiden maintains; that the baptized and sin-
less child might ascend straight to Heaven; and that she might
indeed, as the poem maintains, join the Holy Innocents and the
144,000 virgins who make up the procession of the Lamb. And the
Church maintained, again in agreement with the argument of
the maiden, that, as a number of commentators on the poem have
shown, the rewards of the saved are not identical, although the
blessings of God in Heaven are shared equally. As Dorothy Sayers
states in an illuminating passage, "there is equality [in Heaven] in
the sense that all the souls alike are as full of bliss as they are capable of being: but between soul and soul there is no formal equality at all. The pint-pot and the quart-pot are *equally full:* but
there is no pretence that a pint and a quart are the same thing.

. . ." [36] Thus in the course of the debate the maiden simply does not bother to amplify her point with the glosses of the Fathers; it is in fact doubtful that the persona-narrator, given his bias and limited perception, could have followed her if she had. Her point is that the "grace of God is great enough" to accomplish the salvation and to make rich the reward of even a two year old innocent, and she makes it sharply and effectively.

It is evident also that the poem makes similar use of a number of other medieval traditions. The poem abounds in scriptural and patristical allusions, not only in those passages in which great scriptural scenes are extensively and creatively paraphrased—the parable of the vineyard (Matt. 20:1–16), the vision of the New Jerusalem (Rev. 21:10–22:7), and the procession of the 144,000 virgins (Rev. 24:1–5)—but in numerous scattered allusions and images connected with the description of the maiden, particularly in connection with her raiment, with her arguments, and with the miraculous landscape of the poem.

For example, the allegorical interpretation of the Song of Songs, widely prevalent in the Middle Ages, which saw in the marriage of Bridegroom and Bride the union of Christ and the Church, is reflected in the maiden's description of herself as the bride of Christ (763–64); the pearly crown that the maiden wears reflects a popular medieval hymn;[37] and the river that separates dreamer and child is that which proceeds out of throne of God (Rev. 22:1) as well as the barrier-river of the Other-World romances.[38] In the use of these allusions the *Pearl*-poet follows the usual custom of medieval writers in adapting ancient customs and descriptions to his own time; thus, the New Jerusalem becomes a manor enclosed in a castle wall.

There are some indications also that *Pearl* reflects to a small degree the courtly tradition, a fact that links the poem to *Sir Gawain and the Green Knight,* in which the courtly element is very strong. The dream-vision form itself is that of the *Roman de la Rose,* and the miraculous garden in which the dreamer finds himself is very like that of dozens of Other-World romances. The details of dress, particularly the fashionable wedding gown of the maiden, and of architecture reflect the same intimate knowledge of courtly life revealed in *Sir Gawain and the Green Knight.*

Even the tone of the dreamer's discussion with the pearl-maiden obviously relies upon an accepted code of manners, for it is marked by that peculiarly late medieval view of courtesy which could so blend the canons of secular and divine love as to make their terms, as in "I Sing of a Maiden" and "Maiden in the Moor Lay," almost interchangeable. Thus the Blessed Virgin, the "queen of Courtesy" (432), is in *Pearl* both matchless Mother of God and perfection of the virginal courtly graces; and St. Paul's "grace" by which we are all made members of Christ's body becomes simply "cortaysye" (457).

V *Poetic Techniques*

The verse itself reflects also the poet's acquaintance with the usages not only of the rough-textured alliterative verse of the Anglo-Saxons, but also of the stanza-linking techniques of the imported French forms. The poem consists of one hundred and one stanzas of twelve lines each, arranged in nineteen groups of five stanzas each and in one group, the fifteenth, of six stanzas. The natural supposition is, of course, that one stanza of the fifteenth group, probably either Stanza 72 or 76, is either spurious or was not canceled by the poet. The stanza groups are held together internally by the linking together of each group of verses by the repetition of a concluding refrain and by a device called "concatenation," the repetition of the last word of each verse in the first line of the following stanza.

The individual stanzas clearly reveal both alliterative and rhyming techniques. The basic line is the familiar irregular four-stress accentual line of alliterative verse, but the twelve lines of the stanza consistently follow the rhyme scheme *a,b,a,b,a,b,a,b,b, c,b,c.* This combination of styles of verse, along with the linking of stanzas, results in a metrical pattern of great complexity, perfectly suited to the mixture of formality and personal feeling, of objectivity and deep emotion demanded by the elegy. We are conscious always in the poem of the involvement of the "I" narrator, yet the formal perfection of the poem contains his grief and frees it from bathos.

VI *Narrator and Theme*

But the poet's use of these inherited traditions—allegorical, symbolic, theological, scriptural, courtly, poetic—are all only parts of a whole; and to emphasize any one of them at the expense of the others is seriously to distort both the intention of the poet and the culminative effect of the whole poem. Such interest in the allegorical nature of the maiden and in the peripheral aspects of source and imagery is of course understandable. A poem containing possible allusions to the *Roman de la Rose*, Boccaccio, Chaucer, Dante, and the Vulgate, and utilizing possibly heretical theology, the medieval dream-vision, the elegy, and the *débat* is a critic's land of heart's desire. However, such interpretive scholarship, while undeniably of great interest and value in opening new avenues of critical insight, is nevertheless fragmentary; it is all too seldom directed, except in the most parenthetical manner, toward exploring the total meaning of the poem. We become easily lost in exploring the technicalities of the theology, the possible levels of symbolism in the maiden, and the details of the vision of the New Jerusalem—and are content, therefore, to leave the center of the poem untouched or to murmur that its theme is obvious and pass on.

I suggest that the quickest way to come to the heart of the poem would be to waive entirely for the time being all questions of allegory and symbolism and to concentrate not upon the figure of the girl but upon that of the narrator, whose progress from grief to understanding I have already called the dramatic heart of the poem. For whatever else the poem may be—dream-vision, elegy, allegory, debate—it is, as we have said, a fiction presented from a clearly defined and wholly consistent point of view; we accompany the "I" of the poem through his vision, and through his eyes we see the magical landscapes and the girl. We are never allowed to see and judge the experience presented by the poem objectively and for ourselves; but instead, we are forced, by the point of view which the poet adopts, to accept the experience of the vision only in terms of its relationship to him. The mind of the narrator in *Pearl*, like the mind of Dante the Pilgrim, is the real subject under consideration. It is with the figure of the narrator alone in an "arbor" that the poem begins and ends; it is he who controls the argument with the pearl-maiden by introducing the subjects for debate and by directing the path of the discussion with his questions; it is for his benefit that the maiden relates the parable of the vineyard and allows him to view the New Jerusalem.

The girl—to most critics the center of attraction simply because of her enigmatic and apparently shifting nature—is not introduced until line 161 and does not become actively engaged in the poem until line 241, when she is addressed by the narrator. She then disappears at line 976, to appear only once thereafter in a single reference within the vision of the New Jerusalem. In a poem of 1,212 lines, the girl herself is on the scene for only 815 lines and can be said to participate in the action for only 735 lines, a little over half the length of the poem. Moreover, the pearl-maiden cannot be said to function, except peripherally, in the narrative movement of the poem. During that middle section of the poem which she seems to dominate by her presence, the poet never allows us to lose our sense of the narrator's presence. We know that he is there and listening carefully, interjecting questions and remarks from time to time. We are constantly aware of the fact that it is his consciousness which is directly affected by her remarks. In short, the poet has so constructed the poem that it becomes obligatory for the reader to judge the figure of the pearl-maiden not in isolation but entirely in terms of her relation to the narrator, the "I" of the poem.

The effect of this fact upon interpretation seems to be twofold. First, it forces the reader to regard the action of the poem within the implied dramatic framework which the poet provides; and, second, it requires the reader to fit into that framework all the details, however seemingly unrelated, which the poet introduces —most significantly, the parable of the vineyard, the debate over grace and merit and the ensuing description of the place of the innocent in the heavenly hierarchy, the girl's description of her life in the New Jerusalem, and the vision of the New Jerusalem which is given to the poet.

The poem begins, as we have seen, with a direct statement by the poet-narrator that he has lost "in an arbor" (9) a certain pearl of great value, one which is to him without peer in all the world. He is so terribly grieved by the loss of the pearl that he cannot forget his former delight in possessing the gem; he laments his loss, bidding his "sorrow flee, / And [his] fair fortune turn again" (15-16). But his grief takes another form also: it brings into his mind a series of paradoxes concerning the relationship of beauty and death or, more specifically, of growth and death. He knows that he sang "never so sweet a song" (19) as that which he sings now in his hour of deepest grief; he reflects that the pearl's presence in the earth of the arbor will cause "fair flowers, golden and blue and red" (27) to prosper over her grave; he knows that "the blade grows where the grain lies dead" (31).

In short, the narrator's grief-stricken statements reflect more than personal sorrow over the loss of the pearl. In his grief he begins to consider the paradoxical nature of the universe in which he lives, a universe in which the decay of the body contributes directly to the beauty of nature, where no "flower nor fruit have withered / On turf wherein such treasure lay" (29-30). Like Shelley in "Adonais," he wonders how:

> The leprous corpse, touched by this spirit tender,
> Exhales itself in flowers of gentle breath;
> Like incarnations of the stars, when splendour
> Is changed to fragrance, they illumine death
> And mock the merry worm that wakes beneath.

Having established the narrator's grief and, more importantly, this questioning of the nature and justice of the universe which his grief inspires, the poet begins the dramatic movement of the poem. The narrator states that he has come to "that spot" (49) where he lost the pearl; he has come there, moreover, in the very midst of August, when all growing things have blossomed, when the corn must be cut and the flowers—gillyflowers, ginger, gromwell, and peonies—are "bright and sheen" (42). Here, in the midst of joy, his sorrow becomes even more acute; and in spite both of "reason," which offers only the most temporary relief to his "sudden sorrow" (51), and of the "comfort of Christ," his "will in wretchedness was lost" (55). In this mood, his vision begins.

Thus in the first section of the poem we are introduced, even before we know that the poem is to take the form of a vision, to two facts about the situation of the narrator. First, we learn that he is overcome with inconsolable grief, and from the allusion to the "mound" (41) we judge that the poet is grieving over the death of a loved one. Second, we learn that his grief has taken the form of an awareness, almost of an indictment, of the mixed nature of the world. Standing amid the joyful flowers of August, he can think only of death and of the fact that the rotting body of his beloved child, "so clothed in clay" (22), has produced this profusion of color. The two are so connected in the mind of the narrator, moreover, that his last thoughts upon going to sleep are of his own "wretched will" and, paradoxically, of the fragrance which springs into his senses as he falls asleep. In short, the narrator's immediate grief has developed at the very beginning of the poem into a pondering of universal problems of life and death.

This questioning of the nature of things introduced at the outset occupies the narrator throughout the poem. In order to assuage his grief, he must thus accomplish a reconciliation of the apparently dual nature of heavenly justice. And it is precisely this struggle for understanding which gives the poem its permanence and its enduring appeal. We are seldom, if ever, satisfied with a purely occasional poem; and an elegy which records only a particular grief never becomes in any way meaningful to us. In the great elegies, however, the poet's grief is made universal and thus meaningful by exactly the process we see at work here in *Pearl*. The reader's attention is directed by the elegiac poet not toward the figure of the deceased, but toward the poet's own struggle to accept his loss and, more importantly, toward his struggle to understand in universal terms the final meaning of death and the conditions under which death may be meaningful to him. In "Lycidas," we remember, we are not allowed to become interested in the figure of Edward King. Our attention instead is focused from the beginning upon the struggle of the young Milton, first, to accept the possibility of his own premature death and, second, to understand, in both personal and universal terms, the significance of King's death. Likewise, in "In Memoriam" the figure of Arthur Hallam moves out of our consciousness as Tennyson explores the terms upon which he can accept a traditional faith in a skeptical age. "Adonais" and "Thyrsis" are more concerned with the struggles of the living Shelley and the living Arnold than with the praises of the dead Keats and the dead Clough.

And so it is with *Pearl*. The first section of the poem introduces the narrator's struggle to reconcile the apparent contradiction expressed for him in the contrast of the flowers and the corpse; stanzas II-V introduce the means whereby he can approach a resolution of that contradiction. From the side of the grave his "spirit springs into space" (61) and his body "sleeping lies" (62). He finds himself in a strange world, far removed from the familiar earthly garden where he fell asleep; he knew "not what might be the place" (65). He sees about him the items of the natural world —cliffs, forests, trees; but these familiar sights are transformed

into strange shapes and materials: crystal cliffs, forests filled with
"radiant rocks" (68), silver leaves, and pearls scattered about as
gravel. This is the Earthly Paradise, where the ordinary natural
objects of earth are displayed within and altered by a supernatural context. As Wendell Stacy Johnson points out, the images of
the garden reflect a brightness and light coming from outside
themselves.[39]

Yet even this vision is not the ultimate perfection. Across the
stream by which he walks lies the Heavenly Paradise, the complete antithesis of earth. The images pass here from "the vision of
nature arrayed in (reflecting) light to one of a land and a person
[the pearl-maiden] set in gems and adorned by the 'inner' lightness." [40] Both gardens, however, have a recuperative effect upon
the narrator; the first "inspired in [him] bliss, abated [his] grief, /
ended [his] anguish, destroyed [his] pain" (123–24). But the
second paradise, that which lies across the stream, seems even
more wonderful to him; there, he feels, lies the answer to his di-
lemma:

> For Paradise, the very place,
> Must be upon that farther side;
> The water by a narrow space
> Pleasance from pleasance did divide.
> Beyond, on some slope undescried
> The City stood, I thought, wherefore
> I strove to cross the river's tide.   (137–43)

But the water is deep; and, in spite of his longing, the narrator
cannot cross.

The narrator has now reached a position midway between
earth, with its unsolvable riddles of life and death, and Heaven,
where all contradictions are united. In mythical terms, the narrator has arrived at a testing point; he is midway in the hero's myth-
cal initiation cycle from earth to the strange land of adventure to
earth again. Having accomplished the necessary journey to a
strange land, having accepted the "call to adventure," [41] he finds
his mind "radically cut away from the attitudes, attachments, and
life patterns of the stage left behind [his normal earthly life]." [42]
In the more familiar terms of Arnold Toynbee, the narrator has
accomplished a "withdrawal" from society which "makes it possible for the personality to realize powers within himself which

might have remained dormant if he had not been released for the
time being from his social toils and trammels." [43] Within the context of the poem, the narrator is at a point midway between problem (the apparently paradoxical nature of death) and solution
(the resolving of that paradox). His world has become neither
earth nor Heaven but a middle ground where earth and Heaven
can, under certain conditions as in the dream-vision, meet. In the
midst of his wonderment, just as he is about to attempt a crossing,
he sees before him, on the other side of the stream, the lost pearl;
and, at this point, the debate begins.

What I have just called the "debate," which is to say simply the
conversation between the narrator and the pearl-maiden, falls
conveniently into four parts: (1) the parable of the vineyard, (2)
the girl's discussion of the relative grounds of grace and merit as
means of salvation and her ensuing explanation of the place of the
innocent in the heavenly hierarchy, (3) her description of Our
Lord's suffering in the Old Jerusalem and of her life with Him in
the New Jerusalem, and (4) the vision of the New Jerusalem. To
me, these episodes in the discussion are not digressions used either
for their own sakes or for purposes of general instruction; they are
well-defined and climactically arranged stages in the process by
which the narrator is made to understand the meaning of the girl's
death and so is freed from the burden of his grief. My general
thesis is that the long debate between the narrator and the girl is
the only means by which the narrator can resolve the paradox of
beauty and decay, of growth and death, which has troubled him
and, by that resolution, come to accept the death of his daughter.

It becomes quite clear in the course of the conversation between the living narrator-poet and the dead maiden that their
differences are profound. He is a man, she a saint; and the nature
of the stream that divides them and the function of the vision
itself become clear within the context of those differences. Earth
cannot receive her; he is not ready for Heaven. The debate in
which they engage thus becomes a contest between two points of
view, the earthly and the heavenly, between a point of view
which sees natural death only as an irreducible paradox of decay
and growth and a point of view which can reconcile that paradox
in terms of a higher unity. Thus the terms of the central episode of
the debate—grace and merit—are of no great consequence in
themselves, but have meaning within the dramatic framework of

the poem only as they relate to the attitudes which they serve to reveal in the course of the talk.

Wendell Stacy Johnson has already shown, by means of a careful study of the imagery of the poem, that *Pearl* involves "an emphasis upon a ubiquitous sense of contrast between the nature of heaven and the nature of earth, the revelation of which seems, in [Johnson's] present reading, to be the poet's main purpose." [44] I agree with Johnson's demonstration of the contrast between earthly values and heavenly values, but this contrast seems to me to constitute only the means used by the poet to attain a yet higher end. The narrator's earth-bound nature, which we, as readers, share, and which causes him to balk and quibble at each of her explanations, is in reality the source of his discontent. The girl's purpose in the debate is thus not primarily to prove to him the theological validity of the saving doctrine of grace, but to demonstrate to him a point of view which will allow him to accept the differences in their attitudes and, through this acceptance, to come to a realization of the meaning and purpose of her death. To show the successful resolution of the two points of view exhibited in the poem and, through this resolution, the concomitant acceptance by the narrator of the fact of death thus becomes the main purpose and theme of the poem.

To chart briefly the progress of the argument, the narrator begins with the most natural of questions, a question which stems from his own interrogation of the justness of God and from his earthbound point of view:

> "O pearl," I said, "in pearls bedight,
> Art thou my pearl for which I mourn,
> Lamenting all alone at night?
> With hidden grief my heart is worn.
> Since thou through grass didst slip from sight,
> Pensive and pained, I pass forlorn,
> And thou livest in a life of light,
> A world where enters nor sin nor scorn.
> What fate has hither my jewel borne,
> And left me in earth's strife and stir?"   (241–50)

If both the tone and substance of his question reveal his earthly point of view, the tone and the substance of the pearl-maiden's answer reveal the gulf between them:

You tell your tale with wrong intent,
Thinking your pearl gone quite away.
Like a jewel within a coffer pent,
In this gracious garden bright and gay,
Your pearl may ever dwell at play,
Where sin nor mourning come to her;
It were a joy to thee alway
Wert thou a gentle jeweler.   (257–64)

As E. V. Gordon has said, "In the manner of the maiden is portrayed the effect upon a clear intelligence of the persistent earthliness of the father's mind: all is revealed to him, and he has eyes,
yet he cannot see." [45] The narrator, as quick to be comforted by
the girl's answer as he was by his first glimpse of the Earthly Paradise, suggests that he join her by crossing the stream. She replies,
as of course she must, that he is "mad" (290). The narrator, at this
point, though professing to understand the blessed state of the
girl, quite obviously can interpret their relationship only in the
familiar terms of earth, a sort of relationship which to her can no
longer exist. He is human, he has our sympathy, but he is still
completely dominated by earthly standards. The pearl-maiden
must thus rebuke him, reminding him of his status as a living
man:

Whate'er thy doom, dost thou complain
As man should speak to God most high?
Thou wouldst gladly dwell in this domain;
'Twere best, methinks, for leave to apply.
Even so, perchance, thou pleadest in vain.   (313–17)

The first section of the argument, a sort of prelude to the debate
proper, thus establishes the nature of the differences between the
narrator and the maiden. He asks pity; she demands full understanding; but neither can grant the other's request or acknowledge the other's point of view.

Then the narrator, in the course of blaming the girl for her happiness at his expense ("A blissful life I see thee lead, / The while
that I am sorrow's mate; / Haply thou givest little heed / What
might my burning hurt abate" [385–88]), questions her right to
the high place which she holds in the heavenly hierarchy; if she is:

A queen in heaven while yet so young,
Too high thou dost thyself upheave.

> Then what reward from strife were wrung?
> What worship more might he achieve
> Who lived in penance morn and eve,
> Through bodily pain in bliss to be? (473–78)

She lived, he says, for only two years; she never learned how to pray, knew neither Paternoster nor Creed. Her position is thus, to the narrator, given to her at "too soon a date" (492). It is at this point in her explanation that the girl replies to the narrator's objections with the parable of the vineyard, in which first and last are paid alike; and she ends her telling of the story with an assertion which serves, significantly at this point, to emphasize the differences between the points of view which separate father and daughter:

> More gladness have I, herewithin,
> Of flower of life, and noble name,
> Than all men in the world might win,
> Who thought their righteous deeds to name. (577–80)

But, at this stage of the poem, the narrator, relying wholly upon his earthly standard of value, cannot begin to accept such a departure from what he considers true justice; and he, matching her appeal to biblical authority with his own, tells her that her tale is "unreasonable" (590). Thus her first attempt at conversion fails since the narrator refuses to acknowledge, or even to recognize, her point of view; instead, he continues to advance earthly standards in opposition to her heavenly ones.

The maiden, however, pursues her case by the only means left open to her; she explains carefully and in detail the relationship between grace and merit and the place of the innocent, "saved by right" (684), in Heaven in order to assert that the grace of God is "great enough" (612) to overcome earthly difficulties and standards of justice based entirely upon merit and "great enough" to allot to each a full share of heavenly grace. Moreover, toward the end of her description of the place of the innocent in Heaven, which concludes the second main episode of the debate, the maiden sharply underlines her point in continuing the debate thus far. She says:

> Harmless, faithful, undefiled,
> With never a spot of soiling sin,—

> For these whom the world has not beguiled
> Gladly shall one the gate unpin.
> There shall that endless bliss begin
> Which the merchant sought, and straight was led
> To barter all stuffs men weave and spin,
> To buy him a pearl unblemishéd.   (725–32)

And she ends her speech by admonishing her father to forsake his
earthly standards: "Then let the wild world rave, / But buy thee
this pearl unblemishéd" (743–44).

The point of her remark, occurring as it does at the end of her
attempt to explain to him heavenly standards of justice, is that the
difference in standards between Heaven and earth is such that the
achieving of the pearl (here plainly symbolizing beatitude) demands a complete renunciation of wealth and hence earthly
standards of wealth. That the narrator is beginning to see the
point of the girl's remarks is evident in that, for the first time in
the poem, he himself seems to perceive the nature and width of
the river which separates them:

> O Pearl unblemished, in pure pearls dressed,
>
> . . . .
> Who formed thy figure and thy vest?
>
> . . . .
> For thy beauty, above nature's best,
> Passeth Pygmalion's artifice;
> Nor Aristotle the lore possessed
> To depict in words so fair device.
> Than fleur-de-lys thou art fairer thrice,
> Angel-mannered and courtly bred.   (745–54)

Gordon, in his edition of the poem, notes of these lines that they
are reminiscent of a passage in the *Roman de la Rose* "where it is
argued that neither the 'philosopher' . . . nor the artist, not even
Pygmalion, can imitate successfully the works of Nature." [46] But
this is plainly not the function of the comparison in this context.
The narrator of *Pearl* seems to realize for the first time the fact
that the maiden before him is no longer the girl he knew on earth
as his daughter. Her beauty is a new, an unnatural, beauty; her
face and color derive from supernatural sources and from a realm
of experience which even Aristotle, who catalogued all the forms
of natural things, left untouched. Thus the parable of the vineyard

and the discussion of grace and merit and of the place of the innocent in Heaven are by no means digressive in character; they are integral to the movement and purpose of the poem as the first steps in the process whereby the narrator comes to understand— or if not to understand, at least to accept—the heavenly point of view which the pearl-maiden represents.

But, in spite of this sudden revelation of the central meaning of the maiden's speech, the narrator cannot as yet apply to his own situation the lesson he has apparently learned. For, at the maiden's statement that Christ has "clothed [her] in pearls unblemished" (768), he reiterates his argument that she is unworthy to surpass those women who "for Christ have lived in strife and care" (776); and so he reopens the discussion.

The maiden's third attempt to assuage her father's grief by explaining to him the differences in attitude which separate them takes the form of a description of Christ's sufferings in the Old Jerusalem and of her life in the New Jerusalem. Again, her point is the same, that heavenly standards are not earthly ones, but this time she deals directly with the paradox which lies at the root of the narrator's difficulty:

> Though round our corpses the clay clings,
> And though ye mourn us without rest,
> Knowledge have we of goodly things.
> Through the first death our hope we test;
> Grief goes; at each mass we are blest. . . .   (857–61)

Upon hearing this statement, the narrator comes closer than before to a true and lasting understanding of their differences:

> Behold, I am but dung and dust,
> And thou a rare and radiant rose,
> Abiding here in life, and lust
> Of loveliness that ever grows.   (905–8)

He realizes, in short, that his world of "dung and dust" is forever separate from the one "by this happy bank." Yet, for one last time, he cannot resist asking a favor: he would see the New Jerusalem himself. The reasons for his making such a request again stem from his earthly point of view. He has looked about on the other side of the stream and has seen no hint of "castle wall, / Nor

manor where [the girl] may live" (917–18). He has seen only
"these fields" (921), and he knows with all the dogmatic surety of
earth that Jerusalem is *really* "in Judea" (922). It is the most natural of requests for him. He has come, by now, largely to accept
the girl's point; he realizes that out of "dung and dust" may come
a "radiant rose" and that even though the mysteries of Heaven are
forever incomprehensible to Man, yet death, even his daughter's
death, has a place in the divine plan, however unknowable it may
be. And yet, he is still a man; and seeing is, after all, believing.
And so the vision follows.

The vision, the final step in the process by which the narrator
comes to understand the meaning of death, involves, as did the
parable of the vineyard, the debate on grace and merit, and the
description of life in Heaven, the distinction between earthly and
heavenly standards of value. Here, in the New Jerusalem, the separation is complete; there is no need of earthly light or even of
earthly religious forms:

> Sun nor moon shone never so sweet
> As the full flood of that bright stream;
> Swiftly it swept through every street,
> Untainted did the water gleam.
> Chapel nor church mine eyes did meet;
> There is no temple as I deem;
> The Almighty is their minster meet,
> The Lamb their sacrifice supreme.   (1057–64)

The climax of the vision, and of the poem, comes when the
narrator perceives, with his own eyes, his "little queen" (1147)
sitting among her peers, happy and again "with life" (1146),
though a different kind of life from that he had first wished for
her. And with this vision of an existence forever separate from
earth, all his doubts disappear. In an ecstasy, he wishes to cross
over to her; but he is awakened from his dream and finds himself
again in the garden, his head upon the grave.

It is significant that the narrator's first words upon awakening
show his singlehearted devotion to Christ. "Now all be to the
Prince's will" (1176), he says; and we are to understand, I think,
that all doubts, all challenges, and all questionings have been removed from him. He realizes his own unworthiness to enter as yet
into the heavenly life, his own incapacity to know finally the mys-

teries of the universe. But through a *rite de passage,* he has jour-
neyed to the strange land and has returned, having been initiated
into a new and more meaningful life. He will thus accept the
standards of God, for the most part without understanding, but
also without questioning. It is enough for him; it is "well for me,"
he says, "in my prison-pain / That thou art to the Prince's will"
(1187–88).

Thus, in its treatment of grief, *Pearl* may be in some ways related to the *consolatio,* a form of late Classical and early medieval
literature that, like Boethius' famous *Consolation of Philosophy,*
attempted to instruct the grief-stricken and to offer solace to the
bereaved by justifying to man the apparent whimsicality of Fortune.[47] Originally conceived of as instructional discourses, these
consolationes dealt generally, as does *Pearl,* with what John Conley calls "the sovereign theme of the Christian tradition, as of life
itself: the nature of happiness, specifically true [heavenly] and
false [earthly] happiness"; and it is apparent that in the course of
the poem, the dreamer comes, however slowly and unwillingly, to
accept the finality of the gulf between these two systems of values
as a part of his heritage as fallen man.[48] The poem thus ends with
the narrator's lamenting, not, as before, the death of his daughter
and the corruption of her body, but the corruptness of his own
soul which has kept him from her, and with his prayer that he
may himself eventually be counted among the lowly servants and
"precious pearls" of God.

The theme of *Pearl* is that of most elegies: the acceptance,
through suffering and revelation, of death as a part of the universal plan. In *Pearl,* the parts of the dream-vision become the stages
of redemption. The narrator learns, through a series of trials, to
accept his place among the living. Like Milton's Adam, he can be
said to say:

> Greatly instructed I shall hence depart,
> Greatly in peace of thought, and have my fill
> Of knowledge, what this vessel can contain;
> Beyond which was my folly to aspire.
> Henceforth I learn that to obey is best,
> And love with fear the only God.

CHAPTER 3

Patience

IT is not surprising that so little critical effort has been expended on *Patience*, the third of the four poems of Cotton MS. Nero A.x.[1] The poem is to all appearances a straightforward homiletical poem in which the Jonah story, translated from the Vulgate with but few important additions, at least in incident and doctrine, is used as a negative exemplum and image of what may very loosely be called "fortitude" or "patience under adversity." Superficially compared with its companion pieces, *Pearl* and *Sir Gawain and the Green Knight*, it is for the general scholar in search of cruxes a very unexciting piece.

Yet *Patience* is for the general reader who comes to it without prejudice a happy discovery. The poem is admirably executed— nicely framed, clear in organization, meaningful at every turn— and is so filled with vivid detail as to place it close to *Piers Plowman* in its graphic picturing of the world:

> He trode the deck, and they their gear uptake,
> Catch up the cross-sail, fast the cables make;
> Winding the windlass, do the anchors weigh,
> Swift make to spar the bowline fast alway.
> Gather the guide-ropes, as the great sails fall,
> To larboard lying, catch the wind withal,
> The blithe breeze, blowing, bellies out the sheet,
> The sweet ship swiftly from the shore doth fleet.   (101–8)[2]

Despite the views of early critics who, proceeding from a reconstructed and purely hypothetical biography of the poet, placed this poem last among his works,[3] more recent scholarship has tended to see it as an early, perhaps the earliest, work of the *Pearl*-poet.[4] Metrically, for example, *Patience*, which is written entirely in alliterative verse, is far less complex than are *Pearl* and *Sir Gawain and the Green Knight*, which exhibit a highly skillful fusing of English accentual alliterative meter and French syllabic rhyming meter. To place *Patience* and *Purity* after *Pearl* and *Sir Gawain and the Green Knight* would mean, as one of the editors of the poem states, that "the author (1) began with an attempt at complete fusion of alliterative metre with Romance prosody; (2) then that the two elements were separated . . . ; (3) lastly, that the rhyming line disappeared in *Cleanness* and *Patience*." [5] While such a progress from complexity to simplicity is possible, it is unlikely.

Nor does an attempt to date this poem more positively help to establish the relative chronology of all the poems. A number of scholars have attempted to demonstrate that a relationship exists between *Patience* and the B-text of *Piers Plowman;*[6] but if the references to patience and poverty in the second version of *Piers Plowman* do point to Langland's familiarity with *Patience*, then the most we can say is that *Patience* was written before 1377. In the light of the fact that *Pearl*, which was almost certainly written after *Patience*, is generally dated around 1370, the *terminus ad quem* of 1377 for *Patience* is really of very little help in fixing its place among the poet's works.

I *The Source*

Nor does the poet's use of his source material really tell us much, except perhaps to indicate a relatively early date. The major source of the poem is, of course, the Old Testament Book of Jonah in the Vulgate Bible, and the account of the tribulations of the prophet Jonah is strictly followed by the poet. As in the scriptural story, the poet's account begins with God's commandment to Jonah to go to the Gentile city of Nineveh and to "cry against it." Jonah, fearing the wrath of the Ninevites, attempts to escape God's mission by fleeing to Joppa and there boarding ship for Tarshish. God, however, sends a tempest against the frail ship; and the captain, suspecting that Jonah is the cause of the storm, wakens the prophet and, upon Jonah's confession, has him cast into the sea. "Now the Lord had prepared a great fish to swallow up Jonah. And Jonah was in the belly of the fish three days and three nights," [7] after which, by virtue of his prayers for deliverance, he is spewed up onto the land.

There follows in both Scripture and poem an account of Jonah's second commission to go to Nineveh to preach. This time Jonah obeys God and is so successful in his mission that the King of Nineveh himself repents publicly and orders the whole city to follow his example. "And God saw their works, that they turned from their evil way; and God repented of the evil, that he had said that he would do unto them; and he did it not." [8] Jonah, however, is angry at God's decision to save Nineveh and retires to a hut where he may watch the city from a distance. Here God first orders a "gourd," a vine, to spring up to shelter Jonah; and then, on the following morning, He sends a "worm" to destroy the gourd and a hot east wind to discomfort the angry prophet. God again appears to Jonah and chides him for having "pity" on the gourd that was destroyed, while refusing to feel any concern for the thousands of men who would have perished in Nineveh.

At this point both Scripture and poem end. The poet neither adds to nor subtracts from the incidents of the scriptural account; he does not even supply a dénouement to the Bible's abrupt conclusion. He does, to be sure, amplify to some degree the scriptural text; the complaints of Jonah, the storm at sea, and the description of the whale's belly, for example, are carefully and skillfully augmented in the poem by vivid, meaningful detail. There are a few scattered indications also, particularly in the phrasing and in the poet's choice of details, that he may have had before him a short poem of Tertullian's, *De Jona et Ninive;* but the influence of the Latin poem, if indeed he did use it, is almost negligible.[9]

But although, as we shall see, the poet infuses the old story with new emphases and meaning, nowhere is there present the kind of creative freedom with source material that distinguishes his other works—the amalgamation of theology and poetic convention and feeling that gives to *Pearl* its special tone, or the fusion of the two literary motifs joined for the first time in *Sir Gawain and the Green Knight,* or even the combination of Old Testament narratives in *Purity.* The natural conclusion would seem to be (presuming the four poems to be by a single author) that we are here dealing with a relatively young writer who is content to amplify rather than to add materially to his sources.

The content of the poem, when compared with that of *Pearl,* seems also to testify to the relative inexperience of the poet. As we have seen, *Pearl* is filled with discussions of doctrine which are, if not heretical, then certainly non-orthodox; and these are used with great originality as part of the dramatic structure of that

poem. Like *Pearl, Patience* is also concerned with matters of doctrine, most particularly, as one would expect, with the relationship
between God and Jonah, between demanding master and reluc-
tant servant. And the conclusion that *Patience* reaches is, as we
shall see in detail a little later, essentially that of *Pearl:* that Man
had best "be steadfast and patient in both pain and joy" (525)
and endure patiently whatever misfortunes may fall in the firm
hope that happiness will follow sorrow (5) and in the certain
knowledge that complaining serves only to intensify, never to re-
lieve, pain (53).

But, though both poems deal with the necessity of Man's hum-
bly accepting the vicissitudes that Heaven sends, *Pearl* does so
with a dramatic force never approached in *Patience.* The biblical
narrative, powerfully told as it is in the poem, cannot approach
the pathos of the father's grief for his lost child. Even the most
sympathetic reader cannot identify himself with the ill-tempered
Jonah, "all joyless and carping" (433) to the very end, as he can
with the dreamer in *Pearl,* who is able to rise above his first mis-
givings and to accept upon faith and, without really understanding them, the judgments of God. *Pearl* may be thus seen not only
as a restatement of the essential truth presented negatively in *Patience,* but as a dramatic intensification of it.

This brief comparison should not, however, be taken as in any
way derogating either the artistic merit of *Patience* or the originality of its author. For the attention of the poet is not here directed,
as it is in *Pearl,* toward the dramatic development of character—
which is in *Pearl* largely a matter of elegiac tradition, just as the
story in *Patience* is largely a matter of scriptural tradition—but
upon the retelling of a familiar story, both for its own sake and for
the sake of its immediate application to life—for its "sentence" as
well as for its "solas." And on these two levels, the poem is a
great success. Vivid detail follows upon vivid detail—the ship is
launched with a great flourishing of ropes and sails; the storm at
sea almost swamps the small ship and succeeds in shattering the
mast; the whale's belly is cavernous and foul. And everywhere, as
in the scriptural source, the message of the tale is apparent: "Did
not Jonah once in Judea perform such a trick?" (57) the poet asks,
and proceeds to show how Jonah, through his lack of patience and
humility in refusing to do God's bidding, continually brings upon
himself the judgments of God.

II *Imagery*

Moreover, the imagery of the poem constantly supports and advances this major theme of flight and judgment. As Fr. Edwin Cuffe has pointed out, the poem is filled with images of the "forces and irrational creatures of Nature" [10]—particularly the winds, the whale, and the worm—which are seen within the poem to act as "avenging instruments of God" used by the Almighty to seek out the escaping Jonah. These "mindless creatures are thus personified as the obedient servants of God" [11] and are contrasted with the disobedient Jonah. The poet makes use also of a great number of images of tricks, traps, and games which illustrate the "devices or 'tricks' used by God in the 'battle of wits' " [12] with Jonah. There are also subsidiary images of sleeping and waking, of house and bower, and of clothing, winds, the sowing of seed, flight, and hiding. And all these images unify the poem and give life and vitality to the narrative.

The principal image of the poem, as well as its greatest symbol, is of course the figure of Jonah himself, "all joyless and carping." He is in the poem presented as a negative image of what the poet calls "patience," by which he means something very close to "humility," the ready acceptance of God's mission for the individual, however unpleasant that mission may be. This is in itself a rather startling use of the familiar biblical character; for, although the Book of Jonah certainly contains within itself the seeds of such an interpretation, it was seldom so read in the Middle Ages. Job, positively considered, was the usual Old Testament symbol of patience, not Jonah. Jonah, on the other hand, was almost universally considered by the Schoolmen as a type of Christ and is so presented in a number of patristical works.[13] A series of illustrations in a fifteenth-century *Biblia Pauperum*, or *Poor Man's Bible*, presents Jonah in the whale's belly, along with Joseph in the well, to prefigure Christ's descent into hell; and Jonah's being spewed out upon the land, along with Samson's destroying the temple, to prefigure Christ in His triumphant Resurrection. Such pieces of medieval iconography as these—and like examples in the windows of the cathedrals at Bourges, Le Mans, and Lyons—demonstrate clearly that Jonah was generally regarded not only in the patristical, but also in the popular, tradition as a precursor of Christ.

This view of Jonah, moreover, has its authority in Scripture. When asked "for a sign," Our Lord Himself would give only "the sign of the prophet Jonas": "For as Jonas was three days and three nights in the whale's belly; so shall the Son of man be three days and three nights in the heart of the earth." [14] Thus the Fathers, in their usual manner of treating the events of the Old Testament as prefigurings of the truths of the New, commonly point out, that, just as Jonah remained three days in the belly of the whale, Christ remained three days in the tomb; and, just as Jonah was cast up alive after his confinement, so Our Lord emerged victorious from the grave.

Of this usual medieval interpretation, however, the poet surprisingly makes very little use.[15] Instead, he seemingly almost deliberately avoids what would have seemed to his audience the obvious interpretation of Jonah in order to concentrate on what seems to be a highly original conception of Jonah as a negative image of patience. And as we have seen in *Pearl* and shall see in *Purity* and *Sir Gawain and the Green Knight*, this is quite his usual strategy. In *Pearl*, for example, we remember that, although the poet makes tremendous use of the traditional associations of the pearl (with virginity, with the Blessed Virgin, with *gentilesse*), the identification of the pearl with the grief-stricken narrator and the use of its personification as a dramatic means of assuaging that grief is entirely his own. In the same way, although the stories of *Purity* are entirely scriptural, the interweaving of these stories into a complex mosaic of theme and echo is not in the least suggested in the Bible and is entirely of the poet's own conceiving. Thus *Patience* records not merely the familiar story of Jonah and the whale, but that tale transformed by imagery and emphasis into "a tale of Jonas pitted [not] against merely blind forces, but against the purposeful servants of a deliberate and infinitely clever Hunter." [16] Thus, by inversion, the poem becomes a plea for humility and patience in accepting without question or rancor the commandments and burdens of God.

Such an interpretation emphasizes also the penitential nature of the poem. One recent student of the poem has in fact suggested that *Patience*, as well as *Purity*, is primarily instructional in nature, its purpose being to illustrate the sin of pride and its cure.[17] Jonah's principal sin in *Patience* becomes pride, rather than simply disobedience; and its principal remedy is Dread, the first

of the so-called "Gifts of the Holy Ghost." Thus Jonah enacts a
cycle of sin and repentance through Dread (the prayers inside the
whale's belly), only to sin again in his anger at God's decision to
spare Nineveh.

III *Narrator, Exemplum, and Theme*

Whatever particular emphasis one wishes to bring to the poem,
however—and there is no reason why the poem cannot contain all
of them—it is worth noting in considering the poem in detail that
Patience consists of more than the tale of Jonah; the Jonah story,
like the Pardoner's tale of the three revelers, is structurally an
exemplum set in a sermon, and we would be unwise in either case
to ignore the context in which the exemplum is set.[18] Any sermon
assumes the active presence of a preacher, and *Patience* is no ex-
ception. And although this particular preacher, the narrator of the
Jonah story, is never actually involved in the action in the same
way or to the same degree as is the narrator in *Pearl*, he is certainly
actively present in the poem; and the reader is from time to time
made aware that he is listening not to an impersonal and omnis-
cient author, but to a narrator who, although not strongly individ-
ualized, is nevertheless a man of firm opinion. "Patience is so appointed that it often displeases," the poem begins and ends; and,
in between these two statements of the poem's moral axis, the
narrator-preacher argues from both authority and experience by
asserting time after time both aphorisms:

> For whoever can endure sorrow, happiness will follow,
> And whoever for sorrow may endure nothing, the more he
>   suffers.   (5–6)

. . . .

> Be steadfast and patient in pain and in joy,
> For he that is too busy in tearing his clothes
> Must often sit ragged and sew them together.   (525–27)

and statements of personal experience:

> But since I am concerned with the problem called Poverty,
> I shall provide myself with Patience and deal with them
>   both.   (35–6)

It is important to note the poet's use of such a moralistic preacher-
narrator, for this device is structurally and therefore thematically

essential to the poem. Structurally, it allows the poet the kind of mixed introduction and commentary that serves him so well in the other poems of the manuscript—the wedding feast in *Purity*, the dream-vision frame of *Pearl*, and the stanzas on the founding of England in *Sir Gawain and the Green Knight*. These framing devices in all four poems provide the poet with opportunities to announce, prologue-fashion, his thematic intentions before plunging into the narrative proper. In this way, the dream of the narrator in *Pearl* can be read in terms of the loss of the pearl-maiden, the story of Gawain in terms of the alternation of "bliss and care" that has characterized English history, and the Bible stories of *Purity* in terms of the sanctity of the chaste life.

Thus, the purpose, the function, the exact reason for the poet's rehearsal of the Jonah story is stated, not so much within the tale itself—though this will provide us with corroborative evidence, to be sure—but more generally and forcibly in the sixty-line preamble to the tale, which is both in its form and in its moralistic tone exactly fitted to the theme and intent of the poem.

However, the preamble is not exclusively intended to introduce the story of Jonah (which is not even mentioned until 1. 57) any more than the opening movements of any sermon are intended merely to introduce the particular exemplum to follow; it instead sets forth in general terms the peculiar virtues of patience and poverty. The prologue falls into four rough divisions: the first eight lines announce the healing, soothing effects of patience upon the sufferer; lines 9–34 deal with the close kinship of patience and poverty; and the last fifteen lines repeat the virtues of patience, this time in relation to the life of the poet, and finally introduce the tale of Jonah.

These divisions are, however, more dialectical than real; for they are closely linked by transitional statements in order to sustain the single, closely argued point that the patient endurance of one's lot, no matter how hard or seemingly unfair it may seem, is the wisest course of life and the most pleasing to God. The narrator's unspoken assumption—and it is a fact which underlies not only *Patience*, but *Pearl*, *Purity*, and *Sir Gawain and the Green Knight*—is that evil and suffering are inevitably a part of life in a fallen world. No matter how virtuous or, indeed, how blessed a man's life may be, he must be prepared for suffering.

Read in this light, the prologue to *Patience* becomes no simple

pietistic homily, but a reasoned statement of faith very like those
to which the poet's other poems bear witness. Since this fallen
world is, at best, an alternation of "bliss and care" where even
a Gawain may fail and where two year old inocents inexplicably
die, albeit to gain glory in heaven, then some weapon against
suffering and, more importantly, against hopelessness and despair
must be provided by God in His wisdom and grace. So it is, then,
that "patience is appointed" by God, even though "it displeases
often." Thus "suffraunce"—patience—assuages hearts made heavy
by scorn, quells evil, and quenches malice (3–4). It cannot remove the ills of the world, but it does allow Man to endure them;
and, since "happiness will follow" (5), endurance is the most Man
can hope for.

But patient endurance of circumstance not only helps Man to
take the blows of fortune that he must inevitably suffer, but also
enables him, to some extent, to avoid further pain: "Whoever for
sorrow may endure nothing, the more he suffers" (6). Thus it "is
better to endure the assault betimes / Than forever to suffer one's
ill." (7–8).

The shift in line 8 to the first-person point of view is both inten-
tional and instructive; it asserts the presence of the narrator-
preacher, and it identifies him as a man who has suffered, as he
believes unjustly, and who has thus some right to have made the
assertions of lines 1–7. He heard once, he recalls, the Beatitudes
read at Mass, and he proceeds to recite them through, beginning
with those that are "poor in spirit" (13) and ending with the patient man who can "direct his own heart" (27). These two virtues,
patience and poverty, are then immediately and repetitively
linked in the stongest terms on the grounds that they are natural
associates; they are "tied in a team" (37), "linked in one form"
(38), "of one nature" (4).

These are perhaps the key lines of the prologue, prepared for
by the long recital of the Beatitudes and by the speaker's use of
the first-person pronoun. They have been used at times by the
commentators to adduce the poet's own poverty, willful or unwill-
ful, and always, by means of quotations, from St. Francis, St. Augustine, various proverbs, and even the Koran, to demonstrate the
fact that patience was regarded in the Middle Ages as a sovereign
virtue for the poor. Yet if this interpretation is sound, the whole

passage, indeed the whole carefully planned introduction, becomes merely a digression, for the exemplum which follows has
nothing to do with material poverty. Whatever Jonah's problems
may be, poverty is not among them.

A second look at the text is instructive. Lines 13 and 27, in
which are recited the Beatitudes of poverty and patience, are
linked by the repetition of the word "heart"—blessed are they that
are "poor in heart" and they that can "direct their hearts." And the
Vulgate, which the poet is clearly following, refers at these places
to those who are *"pauperes spiritu"* and those who *"persecutionem
patiuntur propter iustitiam."* The point is, of course, that a special
kind of poverty and a special kind of patience are here defined. St.
Francis and the Koran to the contrary, the poet is not discussing
poverty of goods, either voluntary or involuntary, but poverty of
spirit, humility, the "readiness," as Hamlet will later call it, to bear
for God's sake whatever painful and humble conditions life may
bring.

And of *this* kind of poverty and patience the poem is indeed an
exemplum. This is what the preacher seems to be driving at in line
37 by the phrase "in the text"; the reference here is almost certainly to the "text" of the exemplum, following as it does the "I
shall provide myself with patience and deal with them both" of
the preceding line. Just as the preacher has forewarned, Jonah,
lacking both patience and "poverty" of spirit, cannot accept with
reasonable faith and trust the task which God sends him; moreover, by resisting them, he brings additional tribulation upon himself.

The narrator, having thus made his point by an appeal to Scripture, becomes markedly personal in applying the doctrine to himself. He says:

> Since I am beset with both Poverty and Patience,
> It behooves more me to suffer them together, to take my
>   lot and praise it,
> Than to curse and invite more trouble.
> If it be my destiny to suffer misfortune, what good
>   are my complaints? (46–50)

Or, if God had commanded him either "to ride or to run or to
roam about" (52), would it not be better to do so immediately,

"in spite of his objections" (54), and so avoid at least the further
"vexation" of God's wrath, than like Jonah "to search for safety"
(58) and so find in the end only further tribulation.

The passage is, first of all, a brilliantly accomplished transition;
the trials of the harassed preacher, going somewhat reluctantly
and certainly unthanked about God's business, lead quite naturally to the parable of the unwilling prophet of the Old Testament. Yet, having discovered the mechanics of the device, we are
still puzzled by the intensity with which the shift is made. It
would have been possible, surely, to have introduced the Jonah
story as a negative exemplum of patience without making use of
the personal references, however vague they may be, of lines 46–
58. And we wonder, further, why this sort of "envelope" was used
at all. The Jonah story surely needed no justification as narrative,
and the poet's telling of the story is sufficiently dramatic and
pointed not to demand an apology.

At the risk of reviving all the excesses of the biographical interpretations attached in the past to these poems, it is impossible, as
I have said, not to find here an echo of both the tone and the theme
of *Pearl*. There, the narrator had also lamented his lot, the loss of
his child, or his faith, or something of overwhelming importance
to him; and, during the course of the poem, he had come to accept
that "destiny" only after considerable "complaint" and "grouching."
I do not mean, of course, to advance such a theory in any except
the most tentative of terms. I should not want to explore, for example, as Bernhard ten Brink and Sir Israel Gollancz felt forced
to do, its ramifications into such problems as the order of composition of the four poems of Cotton Nero A.x. However, it is perfectly clear that we are meant to read the sixty lines of prologue to
the Jonah story as something more than a casual introduction to a
well-known Old Testament story, and that we are to read the story
of Jonah as it exists in *Patience* within the context of the whole
poem.

The narrative itself repeats the point of the prologue at every
opportunity and by two principal means: (1) the elaboration of
scenes suggested but not developed in the Vulgate and (2) dis-
cursive interruptions by the narrator-preacher. Thus, the preacher's main point—Jonah's lack of humility—is enforced immediately by Jonah's response to God's first command, to rise and go to

Nineveh. "Whenas that sound was still, that marvel brought, /
Wrathful he waxed, and angry" (73–74). Jonah is both full of
"wrath" at God's presumption in ordering him about and fearful
for his life at the hands of the Ninevites; and his monologue, beginning with line 75, shows all too clearly his lack of humility, of
"poverty in spirit." His most considered evaluation of the situation
is full of pride and self-aggrandizement: God has singled him out
for punishment and will ignore him when he is presecuted by the
Ninevites. He is determined, however, to outwit God by hiding
in Tarshish since "when he is lost [God] will let [him] alone"
(88). Jonah thus goes to Joppa, "swearing for naught he'd suffer
much pain" (90), the very picture of the complaining fool defined
in the prologue.

The second means of emphasis—and one of the poet's most
pronounced and, I believe, deliberate narrative mannerisms—is
the constant intrusion of the preacher-narrator into the story. The
reason for such a device is apparent in the very first of these interruptions. Having described in vivid detail the embarkation of the
vessel, the poet says:

> As Jonah, never Jew so joyful there,
> Deeming from doom divine afar to fare,
> He deemed that Wisdom which the world did plan
> Had no might on the main to vex a man.
> Ah! Witless wretch, who wouldst from suffering flee,
> In plight more perilous and pain shalt be!
> For fancy false doth flatter him, I ween,
> Samaria shunned, of God he'ld [sic] not be seen.   (109–16)

And having in his usual didactic vein made his point, he turns
immediately to Scripture, quoting a passage from the Ninety-
fourth Psalm.

The function of such expansions and digressions as these is obvious. The poet's commentary upon Jonah's imprisonment in the
whale's belly, his contrasting of the immediate conversion of the
King of Nineveh with the continuing wrath and pride of Jonah,
his great elaboration of the conclusion of the worm and gourd
story as typical of the mercy and loving-kindness of God—all
these are means of emphasizing throughout the tale the point of
the prologue: the uselessness of complaining against the appar-

ent injustice of life, and the need for patience and poverty of
spirit as antidotes to the kind of false pride which leads to
"grouching," which in turn engenders more cause for suffering.

There is, however, perhaps a more general point to be raised
concerning the poet's use of the Jonah story within its homiletic
frame. Not only does he relate the story by means of carefully
controlled tricks of emphasis and additions to the theme, and
hence to the structure, of the sermon, but he is able through images and through a liberal, though never excessive, use of graphic
detail to endow the Old Testament story with the energy and
vigor required of the exemplum, the purpose of which was to en-
liven and enforce "the moral lesson of the sermon by one or more
anecdotes, drawn usually from history or legend, from the experiences of life, from the beast fables," [19] or from a variety of other
sources. Thus the purple passages of the poem—the salty accounts
of the launching (95–118) and the storm at sea (137–62), the
grotesque description of the whale's belly (266–80), the vehement
complaints of Jonah to God—are not digressions, however artistic,
in the progress of the sermon; they are firm and necessary parts
of the exemplum, in which such expansions and elaborations were
both permitted and expected.

Moreover, it should be noted that even here the skill of the poet
is clearly demonstrated. Expected and permitted though they be,
these elaborations of biblical material are both far more original
than those found in the usual exempla and, more importantly,
more obviously thematic in intent. Thus, the happy activity of the
crew and the "happy wind" launching the "sweet ship" underscore
the momentary joy not only of the escaping Jonah, but of any man
whose attempted escape from God's will seems at first successful.
The violence of the storm and the horror of the whale's belly witness the consequences of folly, the judgment and the sorrow that
Man brings upon himself by his opposition to God's will. And the
marvelously articulated expansions of Jonah's complaints portray
the impenitent malcontent, "unhappy and complaining," whose
experience has taught him nothing and whose final word (493–
94) is a bitter denial of life.

Short as it is, the epilogue, peroration really, reinforces the general tone and manner of the prologue. The didactic nature of the
narrator is immediately apparent:

> Be not so angry, good man, but go thy way:
> Be steadfast and patient in pain and in joy,
> For he that is too busy in tearing his clothes
> Must often sit ragged and sew them together.   (524–27)

And the preacher here at the very last again insists on relating the story to his own experience, not, however, as in the prologue, to a past experience, but this time, as would be appropriate in an epilogue, to the poverty and pains of the future. The poem thus ends on a note of quiet resignation, recognizing again the inevitability of pain and advocating the nobility of patient suffering.

The poem thus exhibits both structural and thematic unity, as well as great force and beauty of expression. Although *Patience* suffers by comparison with the other poems of Cotton Nero A.x. it may well be that this poem manifests a more subtle power and beauty than that which illuminates the others.

CHAPTER 4

Purity

PEARL is followed in the manuscript Cotton Nero A.x. by *Purity,* called *Cleanness* by its first editor.[1] It is probably an earlier work than *Pearl,* which precedes it, and a later one than *Patience,* which follows it.[2] It is thus chronologically out of place in the manuscript. Nevertheless, *Purity* was almost certainly composed some time between *Patience* and *Pearl* and bears obvious resemblances in structure, tone, and theme not only to these poems but also to *Sir Gawain and the Green Knight.* Indeed, it can be said almost without oversimplification that *Purity* is a further development of the homiletic technique and structure of *Patience,* a preparation for the ecstatic praise of chastity in *Pearl,* with a foreshadowing of the alliance of chastity and loyalty for which Gawain is to be tested.

Like *Patience, Purity* is homiletic in technique, though it lacks the careful delineation of the personality of the narrator-preacher which so marks the tone of the earlier poem. It also reveals a much more complex sermon structure than that of *Patience,* which consists only of a skeletal theme, protheme, dilation and—with the story of Jonah—a fully developed negative exemplum. *Purity,* well over three times longer, has a theme, a protheme, an extended dilation—the parable of the wedding feast—of over one hundred and fifty lines, and nine negative exempla from Scripture, three of which are recounted at great length and with a wealth of original detail. It is no wonder that the poem has never been in any sense "popular," that it has only recently been translated in its entirety, and that critics have consistently condemned it as ill-proportioned.

I *The Action*

The poem begins, as did *Patience,* with a clear statement of its theme. He who would commend "clannesse," purity, will find fair

forms of speech to aid him, for God is always wrathful with the
unclean who follow after filth, especially the false worshippers
and priests who pretend to do His bidding. For this truth, the
preacher tells us, we have the authority of Christ Himself; and as in
Patience, he quotes the appropriate Beatitude from St. Matthew's Gospel: "Blessed are the pure in heart: for they shall see
God." Then, picking up his own image (12) of the man "clothed
in cleanness," the poet begins an extensive retelling of Our Lord's
parable of the wedding guest who attended his master's feast im-
properly dressed.

The familiar story is, as in *Patience,* elaborately embellished by
a great quantity of descriptive items taken from contemporary
life. We are shown a medieval banquet complete with dukes and
barons, "bachelors" and squires, a steward and a marshal; the
guests are entertained with "mete and mynstrasy noble" (121)
and bade to be "myry." And, throughout the telling of the parable, the poet lays his heaviest stress upon the uncleanness of the
rejected guest's clothing—which here, as in the Bible, is said to
represent his sins—upon his perfidy in attending the feast so at-
tired, and upon the punishment meted out to him.

A transition section follows, which again emphasizes the image
of clothing and which states with clarity and force the fact that,
despite the severity of the punishment meted out by God to sinners of all kinds—the slothful, the vain, the covetous, the proud,
to name only a few from the poet's long list—His most severe
wrath has always been reserved for those who follow "fylthe of
the flesch" (202). He then moves swiftly toward the first of his
three major illustrations of God's vengeance on the unclean, the
story of Noah and the Flood. But, before he comes to the tale itself,
he establishes a narrative pattern for the rest of the poem by summarizing two complementary tales: the falling from grace of Lucifer and of Adam, both of whom are cited as having failed in
"trawthe," in loyalty and obedience to God, and who are punished
by being driven from His presence.

But their hard punishment, the poet tells us, cannot match that
of the sinners against purity; and so the tale of Noah is developed
with the poet's customary addition of many graphic details illustrating the fearful destruction of the impure by the Flood. The
Noah section of the poem ends, as did the parable of the wedding
feast, with a warning against "fylthe of the flesch": since one

"speck of a spot," the preacher tells us, will destroy all our virtues in the sight of God, we must be as clean and unblemished as the "margerye perle" (556).

Another transition section, lamenting the uncleanness of all men both in thought and in deed, leads the poet to an account of the destruction of the wicked Cities of the Plain, Sodom and Gomorrah. Again the tale is marked heavily by allusions to "fylth of the flesch" and by graphically detailed accounts of God's punishment of sexual impurity. As with the tale of Noah, the poet introduces two subsidiary narratives, each dealing with a failure in "trawthe": Sarah's laughter at God's announcement that she will bear a child, and the disobedience of Lot's wife. However, these two stories are presented chronologically as parts of the main narrative—the account of the destruction of Sodom and Gomorrah—rather than (as in the Noah section) as prologues to it. The story of Sodom and Gomorrah concludes with a long description of the horrors of the Dead Sea, which, according to the poet, now marks the site of the corrupt cities.

There follows a lengthy transition, which may be the thematic center of the poem. "Love the Lord" and "Conform to Christ," who is polished like the pearl (1066–68), exclaims the poet; and, in a tone very close to that of *Pearl*, he praises ecstatically the virtues of the stainless Christ and the clean soul, which also is likened to a stainless pearl. Yet even the redeemed soul is ever vulnerable to corruption; and, should one of God's sacred souls fall prey to impurity, His wrath is greater even than against the unreconciled. God thus forbids His own to defile anything consecrated to Him, even the vessels used in His service.

This statement leads the poet to begin the last of his three negative exempla of purity, the desecration of the temple vessels by Belshazzar. This time the poet again achieves some small variation in structure by treating sacrilege rather than impurity as the chief sin of the tale. However, it is clear from the context of the story that the poet is identifying Belshazzar's act of sacrilege with "filthiness of the flesh." The consecrated temple vessels may also be identified with the consecrated souls discussed immediately before the Belshazzar story, as Fr. Edwin Cuffe has suggested.[3] Certainly any defilement of the body is in scriptural terms a desecration of the sacred vessel of God.

Told along with the story of Belshazzar as negative examples of

fealty and obedience are accounts of the faithlessness of Zedekiah
and Nebuchadnezzar. The account of Belshazzar's feast ends with
the vivid scenes of punishment and destruction we have come to
expect, and the poem itself ends immediately after the third narrative with a repetition of the text and with a plea for purity in the
sight of God.

II Structure and Theme

In *Purity*, the poet for the first time uses the techniques of
amalgamation and fusion which he employs so successfully in
Pearl and in *Sir Gawain and the Green Knight*. As my summary of
the poem indicates, the organization of the exemplum section of
the poem comprises three elaborated Old Testament narratives—
Noah's Flood, the Destruction of Sodom and Gomorrah, and Belshazzar's Feast—each of which is accompanied by two rather
sparsely told Old Testament narratives closely adjoining the principal narrative in the scriptural source and illustrating a failure in
"trawthe" (i.e., disobedience or unfaithfulness) in Lucifer and
Adam, Sarah and Lot's wife, and Zedekiah and Nebuchadnezzar. It
is clear, moreover, that the poet not only relates the groups of
stories employed in the poem chronologically by treating them as
parts of the same running narrative, but that he has given them,
as he had done the Jonah story in *Patience*, a new thematic relationship by allowing the themes of impurity and disloyalty to
overlap and complement each other.

On the simplest level, for example, the major narrative in each
group of three contrasts with its two accompanying minor narratives by demonstrating that God's wrath upon the unclean is more
dramatically severe than his punishment of the unfaithful. Lucifer
and Adam are driven from God's presence for their lack of
"trawthe," but all unclean men are horribly destroyed in Noah's
Flood. Lot's wife is turned to salt, and Sarah goes free of punishment, but Sodom and Gomorrah are razed. Zedekiah is led into
captivity, and Nebuchadnezzar driven mad, but Belshazzar and
all his kingdom are destroyed. The poet makes this relationship
amply clear when, at the end of the story of the fall of Lucifer, he
asserts that the Lord was not made wrathful by Lucifer's treach-
ery (230), only to assert later (249–50) that in destroying the
world at the time of Noah He manifested His merciless wrath.

However, these two kinds of narratives are more than simple

contrasts. The major narratives suggest that impurity results from
disloyalty and disobedience. Only Noah among all men is faithful
to God's commandments; only Lot welcomes God's messengers
and protects them against the filthy Sodomites; Belshazzar,
though the point is unsure here, neither regards the clear warning
of God (1503–4) nor does he share the respect of Nebuchadnezzar for the Jewish God and for the temple vessels. In each case,
once the sinner has cast away the bonds of loyalty that bind him
to God, he sinks into the mire of his own "natural" impurity. In
short, the poem does not deal simply with impurity and with disobedience, but with the impurity which stems from disobedience.

This is the poets' first attempt at thematic fusion, a technique
which operates much more fully in *Pearl,* in which the elements
joined are literary traditions—the elegy, the dream-vision, and the
allegory—and in *Sir Gawain and the Green Knight,* in which they
are folk motifs, the Beheading Game and the Temptation. But in
all three poems the elements linked by the poet, whether narratives, genres, or traditions, lead to a fusion of precisely the same
two themes—purity and loyalty. In *Pearl,* the father's dream-
vision of his lost daughter's symbolic purity leads him to "trawthe"
and to a renewed obedience to God. Gawain's total test involves
both fidelity to his word and to his host (the Beheading Game)
and sexual purity (the Temptation).

III   *The Sources*

Purity thus establishes a general organizational and thematic
pattern for the *Pearl*-poet's succeeding works, though, as we shall
see in Chapter 5, his treatment of these themes is far from repeti-
tious. *Purity* also establishes a kind of index of the poet's later use
of sources. As we have seen, *Patience* essentially involved the use
of only one source, the familiar Vulgate Bible of St. Jerome.[4] *Purity,* on the other hand, although its principal source is the Vulgate, makes use of at least three other sources, two literary—Mandeville's *Travels* and Jean de Meun's portion of the *Roman de la
Rose*—and one oral, the common non-scriptural religious folk tradition of the Middle Ages.

The use of these sources illustrates the various ways in which
the poet is learning to supplement his major source with subsidiary materials. Mandeville's *Travels,* the most popular though also
the most wholly fictional of the medieval travel books, provides

the poet with his account of the Dead Sea (1022 ff.) and with the "marvellous ornamentation"[5] of the description of the sacred temple vessels (1439 ff.). In both cases the *Pearl*-poet borrows graphic detail which lifts his work far above the humdrum biblical paraphrase common in his time. The Dead Sea is seen as a pit filled with pitch, "broad and bottomless and bitter as gall" (1022), where nothing may live; a place where lead floats and feathers sink, where trees bear fruits of marvelous color, "red and ripe and richly hued" (1045) with cores of ashes. The temple vessels are marvelously ornate: cups in the forms of turreted castles and candlesticks with pillars of brass and branches decorated with figures of birds.

From popular religious tradition the poet borrows the detailed account of the fall of Lucifer with its localization of his throne in the northern part of Heaven (211), the failure of the raven to return to the Ark because of its discovery of dead flesh (459), the disobedience of Lot's wife in putting salt into the food of the angelic visitors (819 ff.), and Christ's breaking of the bread as evenly as a knife could cut it (1103 ff.). Besides adding vividness and interest to the paraphrase, three of these details supply thematic significance as well. The perfidy of the raven and of Lot's wife are reminiscences of the theme of unfaithfulness in the midst of tales dealing with impurity, and the legend of Christ's breaking the bread is used to enforce the picture of the cleanness of Christ's every action.

When the *Pearl*-poet alludes to Jean de Meun's portion of the *Roman de la Rose*, the allusion is made remarkable by the fact that the poet identifies it by author within the poem (1056 ff.). The passage from the *Roman* paraphrased in *Purity* is a piece of advice given by the Lover's Friend to the Lover, its rather cynically taken point being that the Lover should observe closely the personality of his beloved and then suit his actions accordingly. The *Pearl*-poet, however, allows none of this worldly wisdom to creep into his paraphrase, but recommends the Friend's advice to the Lover to the soul seeking God: "Conform to Christ," he says, "and make yourself clean."

This use of a source passage in *Purity* is of course puzzling, not only because it is identified by the poet, but also because it is so wrenched from its original context in the *Roman de la Rose*. Robert Menner, in fact, states that the poet must not have understood the tone of the original to have so applied the passage in his own poem.[6] However, there seems to me no real necessity for such an assumption; the poet's point may indeed be strengthened by his use of secular allusion within a religious context. Just as the sinful lover, directed by his friend, can approach the pure lady only on her terms, so sinful Man must emulate the pure Christ in order to approach God. The allusion to this highly secular section of the *Roman de la Rose* in the midst of an intensely emotional section of *Purity* helps the poet to reveal by means of a startling juxtaposition of religious and secular images the relation of sinful Man to perfect God.

The use of subsidiary sources in *Purity* demonstrates three of the possible ways in which the *Pearl*-poet uses such materials to complement or supplement his major narrative by adding vivid detail, by supplying a thematic allusion, or by emphasizing the point at hand by an illuminating image. His use of the Vulgate, his principal source for both *Patience* and *Purity*, also needs comment. There can be no doubt that the poet was thoroughly grounded in the Vulgate text. So thoroughly familiar was he with the Scriptures that in many places he interjects into a biblical paraphrase words and phrases from another part of the Bible. Moreover, his general use of the Bible is highly creative. While he never changes the basic sense of the narrative line of a scriptural passage, he is always willing to embellish biblical passages in order to emphasize whatever thematic aspect of the source he wishes to bring out. For this reason, the great majority of his additions are to descriptive rather than to purely narrative passages, although he does not hesitate to expand narration, as in the account of Belshazzar's Feast, and thereby to emphasize his theme. In *Patience*, as we have seen, he adds to his source the long, "grouching" speeches of Jonah which illustrate the prophet's lack of patience and humility. In *Purity* his most extensive additions are to the accounts of the punishment meted out to impure men; such passages are not only intrinsically given to such graphic elaboration, but also carry the major theme of the poem: God's wrathful treatment of the impure.

One of the purposes of the poet's additions to the Vulgate text is to establish a tone of what Menner calls "homely simplicity."[7] Thus the poet almost never brings into the poem the allegorical interpretations of Scripture—for example, the identification of the

Ark of Noah with the Church—with which the Exegetes were accustomed to gloss Old Testament stories. "In Purity . . . [the poet] seems to be less fettered than most homilists by theological doctrine and conventional interpretations, even where these may have been known to him. He often shows himself remarkably independent in his simple and direct application of Biblical stories to spiritual truths, and in such cases he is not at all bound by the accumulated allegorizings of centuries of scholastic exegesis." [8] The tone of the poem is, therefore, never heavily dogmatic or theological, but always fresh and vivid and full of movement; the poet apparently has too much respect for his narrative line and for the simple point to be made to allow them to become allegorical or encumbered with exegetical discussion. In *Pearl,* as we have seen, theology is openly brought to the forefront; but in *Pearl* there is no narrative to be impeded, and the theological discussion is itself a major part of the theme of the poem.

Thus, in general, the *Pearl*-poet translates in a thoroughly faithful, though not necessarily pedestrian, fashion most of the purely narrative sections of the poem, though often without using verbal equivalents of the scriptural terms, and he adds very little to what might be called the "moralizing" sections of the poem. Neither does he seem to be concerned with reducing the Vulgate text. We should note here also the fact that these generalizations hold true also of *Patience* and, apparently—for there can be no really sure conclusions because of the lack of sources—of *Pearl* and *Sir Gawain and the Green Knight.* Certainly in these two later poems, there is little moralizing and in those passages where comparisons are possible (the parable of the workers in the vineyard and the description of the New Jerusalem in *Pearl*) the descriptive elements of the original are vastly extended.

IV *Proportion and Imagery*

This apparent inequality in the space devoted to simple narration as opposed to thematic narration and description is the root of the charges of lack of proportion and design that have been brought against the poem, charges which are seen to be baseless when the overall design of the poem is grasped. One section in the poem, however, needs to be fitted into the overall structure before the proportions of the poem can be accurately determined: the seemingly overdeveloped account of the parable of the wedding feast which serves both as a dilation of the theme and, more pointedly, as a prologue to the exemplum.

As I have noted, the parable is introduced by the image of filthy clothing, which runs throughout the poem as a symbol of moral filth. The poet asks whether any man would not reject from his table a guest with torn and dirty clothing and with his "toes out." Such a guest would be forever and universally unwelcome because of his poor clothes. Thus Our Lord, the poet goes on, tells the story of how a great king invited a number of his friends to the wedding feast of his son. The parable of the wedding feast is then recounted in detail and in such a manner as to include not only the theme of the impurity of the guest who must be rejected, but also the theme of "trawthe" through the actions of the invited guests who are condemned for the excuses they make to avoid attending their lord's wedding (75–76). As in the exemplum proper, the section of the narrative illustrating "trawthe" precedes that illustrating impurity, and it is surely noteworthy that, while the unfaithful friends are not punished for their failure to attend the feast, the unfortunately clothed guest is bound, tortured, and imprisoned for life for his lack of cleanliness.

The point is that the parable of the wedding guest serves as an introduction to the structure of the poem and to both of its themes, and so stands as another indication of the poet's concern with matters of structure and balance, a concern which is as evident in this early work as it is in the highly structured *Pearl* and *Sir Gawain and the Green Knight*. For example, the story of Noah in the Bible does not stress to any great degree the terrible nature of the vengeance which God brings upon impure Man nor does it make the Flood the direct result of sexual impurity. For this reason, as well as to illustrate the breaking of "trawthe," the poet begins the story of Noah and the Flood with Adam's unfaithfulness and proceeds directly from Adam to an account of the sins of the sons of Adam (249–72), which are treated as being purely sexual in nature. Again, the poet begins his account of the destruction of the Cities of the Plain with Abraham and Sarah in order to introduce early into the story the theme of impurity through God's prophecy to Abraham of the destruction of Sodom and Gomorrah. The account of Belshazzar's Feast begins with the captivity of the Jews in the time of Zedekiah not only in order to include the narratives illustrating obedience, but also to point forward through Daniel's prophecies to the impurities of Belshazzar.

As might be expected, the poet points up his principal themes by means of imagery.[9] Throughout the poem, unpleasant sights and smells are associated with impurity, particularly in the Sodom and Gomorrah section, and pleasant objects with purity. The poet also makes extensive use of purification images, particularly those of washing, burnishing, and polishing, and of images of clean and unclean clothing. As pointed out in the summary, the pearl becomes a symbol of Christ and of the pure soul, a fact that obviously links *Purity* to *Pearl*, where of course the pearl symbol is similarly conceived. Natural forces, such as the flood, the rain of fire, and the earthquake, are, as in *Patience*, used by the poet as the "swift and obedient instruments of God's vengeance."[10]

In general, then, *Purity* seems to stand midway in the poet's development. In structure, use of sources, and handling of Scripture it is very much like *Patience*, though much more complex. In its theme, it anticipates *Pearl* and *Sir Gawain and the Green Knight*. Like *Patience*, it suffers by comparison with these later pieces, but its own virtues are considerable. As a homily it has strength and point, and as a poem it displays a great flair for detailed description. That it has been relegated to the vast lists of "minor" works mentioned in literary histories is unfortunate, for it not only occupies an important place in the development of its author, but is a poem of great strength and merit in its own right.

CHAPTER 5

Sir Gawain and the Green Knight

THE crowning glory of the four poems of Cotton Nero A.x. is the last, *Sir Gawain and the Green Knight*.[1] To the literary historian, it is the culmination of the romance tradition which began in the works of Chrétien de Troyes two hundred years before; to the source hunter, the perfect wedding of Celtic myth and English literary genius; to the student of poetry, an unusual linking of accentual and syllabic verse; to the historian, a treasure of information on armor, architecture, and costume; to the linguist, a window into an obscure and interesting area of late Middle English. Even a cursory glance at the enormous bibliography of items devoted to *Sir Gawain and the Green Knight* reveals that every line, indeed almost every word, of the poem has been subjected to the most painstaking analysis from various points of view, not once but many times, and that, like a many-faceted jewel, the poem sheds its light into many a dark corner of our knowledge of the Middle Ages.

But its greatest wonder is that *Sir Gawain and the Green Knight* is not primarily a "scholar's poem." The general reader, even the least literary sophomore, never fails to be excited by the movement and pageantry of the poem. The sudden crashing entrance of the Green Knight, "tall as a forest tree" (137),[2] the agonizing journey of Gawain through the wintry forest of Wirral, the brilliantly-detailed hunts, the seductive overtures of the lady— these, along with the other equally arresting scenes of the poem, capture even the most casual reader. It is not in the least necessary to know the antecedents of the poem in order to appreciate its graces—though that knowledge increases appreciation—and somehow the swift movement of the music of the poem is preserved in even the most prosaic translation. Next to *The Canterbury Tales*, *Sir Gawain and the Green Knight* is our greatest literary heritage from the fourteenth century; and it is as perennially fresh and meaningful.

I *Versification*

A great deal of the effectiveness of *Sir Gawain and the Green Knight* lies in what I have called its "music," in its complex and varied line and stanza structure. The 2,530 lines of the poem are arranged in one hundred and one stanzas varying from twelve to thirty-eight lines in length, each of which concludes with a unique five-line, cross-rhyming "bob and wheel," the "bob" consisting of a single one-stress line and the "wheel" of four three-stress lines. As in *Patience, Purity,* and *Pearl,* the main body of the stanza is alliterative, and much of the metrical tension of the poem results from the play in each stanza between the short rhymed concluding lines and the long alliterative lines, just as refrain and concatenation add interest to *Pearl.*

Sir Gawain and the Green Knight exhibits also a flexibility in the use of the alliterative line unrivaled in Middle English verse. The lines of the poem, for example, are far richer in the number of alliterating syllables than are the usual verses of the period. Whereas the standard alliterative line of the period has three accented alliterative words, two in the first and one in the second half-line, the *Pearl*-poet many times exceeds this minimum by using three accents in the first half-line. He makes use also of a number of other elaborate variations of standard alliterative technique: he often uses two sets of alliterating syllables within a single line; he alliterates voiceless with voiced consonants ("f" with "v," "s" with "z"); and he allows the alliteration to fall on an unaccented syllable, such as a prefix or an unaccented preposition or the second element of a compound word. He sometimes even allows the unalliterated final word of a line to determine the alliterative pattern for the following line.

Such liberties provide the poem with a rhythm patterned and flexible, determined and free. Because of the added alliterating syllables in many lines, the poet is able to use a much longer line than is ordinarily possible, thus permitting him a greater freedom in the placement of accent and so adding interest and variation to the meter. Though the reader may not be cognizant of the actual poetic devices employed by the poet, he is conscious always of the graceful, swinging quality of the verse.

II *The Action*

Part, but only part, of the poem's charm lies in the story itself, the elements of which are far older than the poem. *Sir Gawain and the Green Knight* begins by establishing its own ancestry: Britain, we are told, was founded by the Trojan Brutus, who established a land where "war, waste, and wonder. . . / Have dwelt within its bound; / And bliss has changed to care / In quick and shifting round" (16–19). The most famous of the lineage of Brutus was the famed Arthur, and the poet's immediate intention is "to tell an adventure / Strange and surprising, . . . / A strange thing among all the marvels of Arthur" (26–28).

This adventure took place at Christmas, and the poet proceeds to describe in lavish detail the brilliant celebrations of the court. The great feast culminates on New Year's Day when suddenly in upon the joyous court bursts a great giant, "the hugest of men"; "a splendid man to view / He came, entirely green" (148–49). Beautifully clothed in green and gold and astride a brilliant charger, the bushily bearded giant carries in one hand an awesome ax, but in the other the holly branch of peace. The court is stunned by the appearance of this apparition, but finally the Green Knight announces in answer to Arthur's request that he has come to play a fearful "Christmas game" (282): he will trade ax blows with any member of Arthur's court, the challenger to strike now, the Green Knight to return the blow in a year and a day. When the assembled company remains silent, the Green Knight glowers at them and taunts the awestricken knights:

> "What!" quoth the hero,   "Is this Arthur's household,
> The fame of whose fellowship   fills many kingdoms?
> Now where is your vainglory?   Where are your victories?
> Where is your grimness,   your great words, your anger?
> For now the Round Table's   renown and its revel
> Is worsted by one word   of one person's speech,
> For all shiver with fear   before a stroke's shown."   (308–14)

Arthur comes forward and takes the ax; but before he can wield it,[3] Gawain modestly asks the King's permission to accept the Green Knight's challenge. Arthur agrees, and with his royal blessing Gawain severs the Green Knight's head from his body with a single stroke. The Green Knight, however, quickly picks up his head and mounts his horse. The disembodied head tells Gawain that in a year and a day he must seek out the Green Chapel and there receive his blow; then the Green Knight leaves. Once he is gone, the court gaily returns to its New Year's feast.

As the year passes, the court becomes increasingly apprehensive. Finally, at the Feast of All Saints (November 1), Gawain can delay no longer and, after elaborately arming himself, starts northward on his journey. He travels alone through desolate lands until he finds himself in the Wirral, a forest haunt of bandits and outlaws. Here he must fight not only the natural enemies of Man —snakes, wolves, and bears—but also the supernatural—giants and trolls. And worst of all, he must endure the terrible cold, sleeping at night in his armor on the bare rocks.

On Christmas Eve, in response to a prayer to the Blessed Virgin that he find some lodging where he can hear Mass, he comes upon "the comeliest castle that knight ever kept" (767). Here he is welcomed by Bercilak, the lord of the castle, and his court. They treat him royally and invite him to stay as a guest until New Year's Day, for the Green Chapel is only two miles away. To pass the time, Bercilak and Gawain agree to a game: Bercilak is to hunt each day, Gawain is to rest in the castle; in the evening each will give the other whatever trophy he wins during the day.

The next morning Bercilak leaves the castle to hunt deer. While resting in bed, Gawain suddenly becomes aware that Bercilak's beautiful wife, whom he had glimpsed momentarily in the chapel, has entered his chamber. He feigns sleep, but the lady comes forward and seats herself on his bed. After a time Gawain pretends to awaken. The lady claims him as her prisoner and offers herself to him. Gawain, stunned by these overtures, manages to evade the lady's advances, agreeing finally to kiss her once in parting. Meanwhile, Bercilak has been successful in the field (the poet describes in detail the "breaking" of the deer). On his return, Becilak, in accordance with the bargain, gives Gawain the venison and, puzzled, receives from Gawain a single kiss, his day's trophy.

The second day, Bercilak goes off to hunt boar, while Gawain is again besieged by Bercilak's lady. This time her advances are more open, but Gawain firmly, though courteously, repels her. That evening, Gawain returns to Bercilak the two kisses he had yielded during the day.

The following day, New Year's Eve, Bercilak hunts a wily fox, and Gawain finds himself accosted by a very determined lady; in fact, we are told that were it not for the help of the Blessed Virgin, he might have succumbed to her advances. During their conversation, the lady offers Gawain a girdle of green silk, which she tells him has the property of protecting its wearer from all harm. Gawain, who has become increasingly fearful of the result of his approaching encounter with the Green Knight, accepts the girdle and even agrees to conceal the gift from Bercilak. That night Gawain awards to his host only the lady's three kisses. He bids farewell to his new friends at Bercilak's court and retires to spend a sleepless night awaiting the next day's combat.

Before dawn, Gawain sets out toward the Green Chapel accompanied by a guide provided by Bercilak. Resisting the guide's entreaties to turn back, Gawain goes on until he comes to "a mound, as it might be, / A smooth, swelling knoll by the side of the water" (2171–72), a place where well might "the fiend, when midnight's near, / His matin prayers recite" (2187–88). Soon he hears the dreadful whirring sound of an ax being sharpened; then the Green Knight emerges from a cavern brandishing an ax more fearful than his original weapon. Gawain prepares for the blow, but glancing upward sees the blade descending and flinches. When the Green Knight taunts him for his cowardice, Gawain, smarting from the rebuke, urges the giant to strike a second time. The Green Knight then feints a second blow and, on finding that Gawain's heart is now "whole," strikes his third blow, which merely nicks Gawain's neck slightly.

At this, Gawain promptly offers combat; but the Green Knight reveals himself to be none other than Bercilak, Gawain's host, and explains that his three blows represented the three exchanges between host and guest, the nick on the third stroke being Gawain's punishment for withholding the green girdle. Gawain, overcome with shame, flings the girdle at Bercilak, exclaiming "Lo! there is faith-breaking! evil befall it" (2378). The Green Knight, however, urges Gawain to keep the girdle as a remembrance of their encounter and goes on to explain that the whole game was initiated by Morgan le Fay, whom Gawain had previously seen but not recognized, who wished to test the pride and glory of Arthur's court and in doing so to cause Guinevere to die from fright.

Gawain leaves for Arthur's court immediately and upon his return tells his adventure to the assembled court and with considerable shame shows his scarred neck to all. Arthur and the court laughingly transform Gawain's emblem of failure into a bright baldric of honor. The poem ends as it began with a reference to the fall of Troy and the noble ancestry of the British race.

III *Form and Structure*

It is immediately apparent to the reader who comes to *Sir Gawain and the Green Knight* from the other romances of the period that this poem is far superior in its organization and structure. The romance as such is wholly a medieval form of literature; and, although it has its antecedents in the long narrative tale of the Graeco-Roman tradition and in the Classical and early medieval epic, it is distinctly a product of the chivalric, as opposed to the heroic, society and shows quite clearly in its typical themes and structure the effects of a leisured and elegant audience. Its very name, in fact, comes from the adverbial *romanice,* "in the Roman manner," and so distinguishes it immediately from the more somber works written in the formal Latin cadences.

The medieval romances, the popular literature of the aristocracy, are thus "stories of adventures in which the chief parts are played by knights, famous kings, or distressed ladies, acting most often under the impulse of love, religious faith, or, in many, the desire for adventure." [4] As distinct from their immediate forebears, the epics, they are filled with mystery, courtly love, endless psychologizing, and, most important perhaps, an almost total lack of organization. The epic is tightly constructed, its organization usually fastened to the adventures of a hero who, whatever his wanderings, is propelled by a firm destiny toward an established goal. The hero of the romance generally wanders aimlessly from adventure to adventure, and the initial quest which prompted him to leave his court—the pursuit of a white stag or the report of a princess held captive in some far-off tower—is soon forgotten in a series of encounters with the Black Knight of the Black Lands and the Red Knight of the Red Lands and the Purple Knight of the Purple Lands.

Not all the romances of the twelfth, thirteenth, and fourteenth centuries, however, are quite this aimless in structure. The very first romances, those of Chrétien de Troyes, certainly manifest a keenly defined and original structure, quite unlike anything in the epic tradition. [5] The adventures of Chrétien's knights are not

simply a series of episodes designed to exhibit the prowess of the
hero, but are steps in the hero's progress towards a goal, usually
that of rehabilitation in the eyes of his lady or of society. But later
romancers in the tradition of Chrétien seem never to have followed the pattern implicit in the series of adventures pursued by
Chrétien's knights, and the romance as a type is marked by an
episodic aimlessness in structure, apparently pleasing enough to
an audience which had endless leisure and an insatiable appetite
for details of combat, but irritating to an audience used to coherence and point.

Sir Gawain and the Green Knight stands almost alone in the
post-Chrétien tradition of the medieval romance because it has
coherence and point. Why this should be true, why suddenly at
the very end of the tradition when the romance had become
somewhat passé in fashionable literary circles, there should suddenly appear in the remote back country of Western England
such a perfectly formed, tightly structured example of the genre,
no one can truly say. Perhaps the *Pearl*-poet, despite his obviously
courtly background and his great reading, was never really a "romance writer" and so could view objectively and thus avoid the
inherited weaknesses of the genre. Or perhaps the fact that the
romance form is used by him not simply as an exercise in a particular literary tradition, but as a vehicle for a commentary on life,
endows the poem with a clearly defined organization and helps
avoid the usual aimlessness of the type. At any rate, the structure
of *Sir Gawain and the Green Knight* clearly demonstrates that it is
the product of a genius who has reduced the aimless wandering of
the knight of the romances to a carefully directed quest for salvation.

Even so, the overall structure of the poem has been misunder-
stood to some degree by modern critics. Sir Frederick Madden,
who first edited the poem in modern times,[6] divided the work into
four great sections or "fits," the divisions occuring at lines 491,
1126, and 1998; and the poem has been so divided by every subse-
quent editor. However, as Laurita L. Hill has pointed out,[7] the
poem in the manuscript is itself divided internally by the use of
capital initials of various sizes[8] into *nine* divisions, four of which
coincide with those marked by Madden; the other divisions oc-
cur at lines 619, 763, 1421, 1893, and 2259. It is clear, moreover,
that in the other three poems of Cotton Nero A.x. similar capital

letters are used with the obvious intent of dividing the poems into their natural divisions—in *Pearl*, to mark the famous five-verse divisions; in *Patience*, to separate "the four chapters of Jonah with an introductory prologue," and in *Purity* both to correspond to chapters in the Vulgate and to mark other changes in source. It is therefore highly likely, as Miss Hill points out, that the poem is actually more intricately organized than its editors have indicated. Certainly the division created by the use of capitals within the poem emphasizes far more precisely than does the four-part division the stages of development of the action in that it clearly delineates as entities such sections of the poem as the passing of the year and the journey of Gawain.

Regardless, however, of how many parts one divides the poem into, it is clear that the main incidents of the work are arranged in a perfectly defined and balanced pattern. As Dale B. J. Randall has pointed out, the poem begins with three introductory elements—the reference to the fall of Troy, the account of the founding of Britain by the Trojan Brutus, and the setting of the scene in Arthur's court—elements which are almost verbally repeated, in reverse order, to round out and conclude the poem.[9] Each of the hunting scenes of Fit III is, moreover, developed in the same way: the account of the hunt is itself divided by the interview between Gawain and Bercilak's lady and is concluded by evening festivities. There is evidence also that the poet telescoped the third and fourth days of the Christmas celebrations at Bercilak's court in order to keep the symmetry of the three hunts and the three blows of Bercilak.[10]

Even more strikingly, as H. L. Savage has indicated, the action of the hunts mirrors perfectly the temptations that Gawain undergoes in his bower: like the deer, he is on the first day politic, adroit, and tactful in handling the overtures of the lady; on the second day, he, like the hunted boar, faces his pursuer directly and resists her advances actively; finally, on the third day, to his shame he follows the duplicity of the fox.[11] Professor Savage's theory is amply supported by the heraldry and hunting manuals of the period, which record characteristics of the hunted beasts that would be perfectly familiar both to the poet and to his audience.

The unity of structure is also assured by a number of parallel situations and images whose main function is to draw together the various parts and themes of the poem. In each fit there are festal meals: Arthur's New Year's celebration in I, the welcoming dinner that Bercilak gives to Gawain in II, the courtly dinners at Bercilak's castle in III, and Arthur's celebration at the return of Gawain in IV. Each fit also describes the arming of knights: the Green Knight in I, Gawain in II, the hunters in III, and Gawain again in IV.

Many parallel incidents also serve to make connections backward and forward in the poem and so keep the major action of the work constantly before the reader. For example, the slaughtering of the captured animals suggests the beheading game; the exchange of gifts at the end of each day in the castle and the New Year's gift game at Arthur's court suggest the exchange of blows; each of Gawain's two journeys suggests the other by repetition of the description of the terrain. These, like the descriptions of arms and dress, serve both to maintain structural unity and to establish the background of pomp and splendor against which much of the action takes place.

IV *The Sources*

All of these unifying devices—the division of the poem into a series of interrelated parts, the tapestry-like alternation of parts of episodes, the relating of bedroom scenes to hunting scenes, the use of "chiming" images and episodes—are means of giving strength and internal coherence to what was obviously the poet's chief problem of organization: the fusion of two ancient and oft-repeated motifs of Celtic literature usually referred to as the Beheading Game, or Challenge, and the Temptation.

The first comprehensive analysis of these two motifs in the poem was made by Professor G. L. Kittredge some fifty years ago in a book devoted to the sources of the poem;[12] and, although modern scholars have modified Kittredge's theory in some of its detail, the basic lines of plot transmission laid down by him still stand.

The ultimate origins of both stories are, like all of the stories of King Arthur, lost in the mists of the Celtic oral tradition. Present-day scholarship is more or less agreed that there did exist an historical "Arthur," though certainly never a "King Arthur." The actual Arthur from whose simple deeds grew the vast and complex network of stories associated with his legend was in all probability a Celtic cavalry leader, a *dux bellorum* as his first chronicler calls him, who fought valiantly against the invading Saxon forces in the early sixth century.[13] He is credited in the early chronicles with having killed 960 Saxons single-handed at the great battle of Mount Badon (site unknown), which took place about the year 500; but, since this deed is first recorded some three hundred years after the events recorded, it is clear from the very first mention of the deeds of the valiant Arthur that he was even then more myth than man. He was the heroic creation of a defeated people, those Celts who were thrown by the warlike Saxons back into the extremities of the island, north into Scotland and across the Irish Sea into Ireland, and, most importantly for the Arthur legend, westward into Wales. Here, in Wales, in the social isolation of the next seven hundred years the myth grows: Arthur kills nine hundred and sixty Saxons at Mount Badon, the tombs of his dog and son are said to have magical properties, Arthur battles a giant at St. Michael's Mount, Arthur is said to be a king, a *Rex Britannorum*, with a wife and a great retinue of knights—so the legend developed. Arthur's associates, later to become the familiar knights of the Round Table, are obviously drawn from Welsh folklore and solar myth.[14] Gawain, for example, in the early years Arthur's greatest knight, seems descended from a Celtic sun god; and Arthur's battles may well reflect Celtic fairy lore. Whatever the particulars of their origins, the tales of King Arthur are well-nigh completely formed in the Celtic oral tradition by the time they find their way into written literature in the *Historia Regum Britanniae* of Geoffrey of Monmouth in 1137.

The two stories that join to make up the plot structure of *Sir Gawain and the Green Knight* are parts of this same Celtic tradition and hence their earliest versions are forever lost. Their ultimate patterns, however, can be at least partly reconstructed from a few early written legends which, although they exist in the Irish rather than in the Welsh tradition,[15] almost certainly record variants of the same stories that existed in the Welsh oral tradition.

The first of these stories, the Beheading Game, has the clearest history of transmission. Its first appearance in written form is in an eighth- or ninth-century Irish epic of Cuchulainn (who may well be the same person as the Welsh Gawain) called *Fled Bricend* or *Bricriu's Feast*, though its oral form must be at least a century older. In a portion of this epic usually called "The Champion's Bargain," a magician, Uath Mac Imomain, proposes a be-

heading game to Cuchulainn and two companions, the three of
whom are vying for the "champion's portion." Cuchulainn accepts
the challenge and successfully cuts off the magician's head.
Twenty-four hours later, according to the agreement, Cuchulainn
appears before the magician, who declares the contest finished
after striking three light blows and praises Cuchulainn's great
valor. In another episode of the epic, a savage churl appears at
court and proposes another beheading game. One hero, Munre-
mur, accepts the challenge, beheads the *bachlach*, and then fails
to keep the agreement. Two other heroes also fail to keep the
pledge; but on the fourth night Cuchulainn appears, accepts the
challenge, and returns on schedule to face the churl. The churl
then strikes Cuchulainn once with the blunt edge of his ax, declares Cuchulainn to be the best warrior of the court, and van-
ishes. The bard reveals the churl's true identity—Curoi mac Dairi,
the judge of the "champion's bargain."

At some time between the ninth and the late twelfth centuries,
the Beheading Game motif passed from Irish folklore into the
French romance tradition, though no one has been able to trace
exactly the stages of this early transmission. It appears, however,
in several French romances of the twelfth and thirteenth centuries
—the *Livre de Caradoc, La Mule sanz Frain* ("The Mule without
a Bridle"), *Perlesvaus,* and *Gawain et Humbaut*—works in which
the Beheading Game motif was in all probability derived not directly from Celtic sources, but from a group of earlier French romances now lost.

The story pattern, however, and its relation to *Sir Gawain and
the Green Knight* are perfectly clear. In the *Livre de Caradoc,* for
example, the scene is Arthur's court and the entire action has
taken on a courtly flavor. Arthur is portrayed at his Whitsuntide
assembly awaiting, according to his custom, some adventure.
Soon a knight comes into the hall and initiates the beheading
game. Caradoc responds and is told to be ready in a year to receive a blow in return. The knight returns at the appointed time,
and, when he finds Caradoc waiting, strikes him with the hilt of
his sword and praises his courage.

The other romances in the tradition tell approximately the same
story but with minor variations. In *Perlesvaus,* for example,
Lancelot is the hero, and the detail of the hero's flinching at the

first blow is included. Gawain is the hero of both *La Mule sanz Frain* and *Gawain et Humbaut*.

These brief summaries demonstrate the closeness with which the *Pearl*-poet follows the thirteenth-century romance form of the legend. The relationship of *Sir Gawain and the Green Knight* and *Le Livre de Caradoc* is so close, in fact, that one scholar has claimed *Caradoc* to be the immediate source of the English poem.[16]

The Temptation motif, on the other hand, is more difficult to trace, and its immediate connection with *Sir Gawain and the Green Knight* is much less clear. The Temptation story, like the Beheading Game, almost certainly goes back to Celtic oral tradition, but we have no ninth-century epic to provide an archetypal form of the tale. The earliest example of the Temptation motif is perhaps that detected by R. S. Loomis in the *mabinogi* or bardic tale of *Pwyll,* an early twelfth-century Welsh work; but it is unlikely that it is one of the progenitors of the English poem.[17] The version of the tale closest to *Sir Gawain and the Green Knight* is found in *The Carl of Carlisle,* an English romance written sometime after *Sir Gawain and the Green Knight,* but derived presumably from a lost French original older than *Sir Gawain and the Green Knight.* In *The Carl of Carlisle,* Gawain, as part of a test of his obedience, successfully resists the overtures of his host's wife, who has deliberately been sent to tempt him by his host. In *Le Chevalier a L'Epée* Gawain resists the overtures of his host's daughter, and in *Yder* the advances of his host's wife, though this time he must resort to kicking her in the stomach to protect himself. The presence of the Temptation motif in *Lanzelet,* a twelfth-century German romance, also demonstrates its popularity. However, none of these analogues exhibits the polish and verve of the scenes between Gawain and Bercilak's lady, and it therefore seems fair to assume that the Temptation sections of the poem are largely the work of the *Pearl*-poet.

The greatest single problem concerning the sources of *Sir Gawain and the Green Knight* is that of the way in which the two source motifs were combined. Kittredge believed that the Beheading Game and the Temptation were first joined in a single poem by an unknown French romancer in a now-lost romance, his principal evidence being the fact that a later English version of the

combined stories, *The Turk and Gawain,* seemed to him to have
been derived not from *Sir Gawain and the Green Knight,* but
from a similar combined version, probably in French and certainly
not extant, which he reasoned to have been also the source of *Sir
Gawain and the Green Knight.* Kittredge pointed out that there
are a number of places in the poem where a French original may
be alluded to. The poet says, for example, that he first heard the
story "in town" and that it has long been "in the land" though
"locked in true letters." Later followers of Kittredge's theory have
also pointed out that the courtly tone of the poem and its occasional use of French idiom in expressions like *"cros Kryst"* also
bear witness to the influence of a French original.[18]

J. R. Hulbert, whose work on the poem appeared at almost the
same time as that of Kittredge,[19] believed that the Temptation and
the Beheading Game were originally part of the same oral Celtic
fairy legend, which recounted how Gawain was enticed by a fairy
to her Other World domain, but was entertained by an emissary
before his arrival (the Temptation) and was faced with the Beheading Game as a condition of entrance to the Other World.
However, since Hulbert's theory is almost entirely hypothetical
and can be supported by no written version of the story, it has
gained few supporters.

The most severe modification of Kittredge's theory of transmission has been suggested by Else von Schaubert,[20] whose general
and most attractive theory is that the two motifs were first joined
by the *Pearl*-poet himself. Hence, according to Schaubert, there is
no need to hypothesize a missing French source, for the existence
of which, after all, there is so little evidence in the text. Schaubert's principal argument for the originality of the *Pearl*-poet's
work is that the method of enlarging an existing romance by the
addition of a second plot strain is wholly English in practice and
is to be found in none of the French courtly romances. Thus, concludes Mabel Day, who agrees in substance with Schaubert's theory, "it is not unnatural to suppose . . . that he [the *Pearl*-poet]
went on to combine . . . two stories which had finally the same
moral" [21]—the testing of the ideal knight's courage and faithful-
ness and cleanness.

Yet other circumstances under which the Beheading Game and
the Temptation might have been joined have been suggested.

Alice Buchanan argues that there are strong suggestions of the Beheading Game mixed in with the Temptation theme in *The Carl of Carlisle* and in two other Arthurian episodes, and that the *Pearl*-poet thus needed no combined French source.[22] Laura Hibbard Loomis, on the other hand, finds the two elements combined in the twelfth-century German *Lanzelet,* though she sees no possibility that the German poet ever influenced the *Pearl*-poet.[23]

It is clear, moreover, that many elements of the poem other than the two main plot lines go back to Celtic and other ancient sources. Almost certainly the Green Knight's name, Bercilak de Hautdesert, is a corruption of the Irish *bachlach* ("churl"), a three-syllable name repeatedly applied to the challenger of Cuchulainn in *Bricriu's Feast*.[24] And, as would be expected, the origins of the Green Chapel, the Green Girdle, the pentangle, and particularly the figure of Morgan le Fay have all been found in Celtic folklore.[25] The greenness of the Green Knight has been explained in terms both of its possible connections with early vegetation myth and with its Celtic origins.[26] John Speirs, for example, sees in the Green Knight vestiges of the primitive folk figure of the "Green Man . . . the Jack in the Green or the Wild Man of the village festivals" who is descended from the "Vegetation or Nature God of almost universal and immemorial tradition . . . whose death and resurrection are the myth-and-ritual counterpart of the annual death and re-birth of nature."[27] Francis Berry, following Speirs's line of thought, identifies the greenness of the Green Knight with his strength and "creative energy."[28] R. S. Loomis, on the other hand, sees an explanation of the Green Knight's color in the ambiguity of the Welsh word *glas*, which has been translated as both "grey" and "green," and notes that Curoi, the magician of *Bricriu's Feast,* is referred to as the "man in the grey mantle."[29] Hulbert notes that green is a common fairy color, and Kittredge believed the greenness of the Green Knight to be an ancient feature of the Celtic tale.

Nor does the mythic ancestry of the poem end with its Celtic origins. The great Indian scholar, Ananda Coomaraswamy, found that the Beheading Game had many parallels in Indian myth and ritual,[30] and Heinrich Zimmer, in the midst of a psychoanalytical investigation of the poem, managed to discover in the details of *Sir Gawain and the Green Knight* analogues to the folklore of

East and West alike.[31] The Green Knight has also been identified
with the Lord of Hades, about whom vestiges of the public execu-
tioner still hover,[32] and with a "fende" from hell sent to test a
Christian knight.[33] There have also been efforts, as might be expected, to identify the Green Knight of the poem with an historical
figure. Thus scholars have seen in the poem possible allusions to
one Ralph Holmes, a captain of the White Companies in Spain in
1369,[34] and to one Simon Newton, often referred to as the "Green
Squire." [35] These attempts at identification, however, like the
attempts to link the poem with the founding of the Order of the
Garter,[36] are in the end only hypotheses and have no bearing upon
the literary effects and merits of the poem.

V   *The Poet's Additions*

But, although scholars disagree about the origins of the various
elements of the poem and about the way the basic plot motifs of
the poem were combined, they are somewhat more in agreement
concerning those elements actually added by the English poet.
First of all, the *Pearl*-poet may very well have added that element
of plot which binds together the Beheading Game and the Temptation—the so-called Exchange of Winnings between Bercilak
and Gawain, which, though it appears in the *Miles Gloriosus*, a
twelfth-century Latin poem, is used uniquely in the Arthur romances by the *Pearl*-poet.[37] Not only does the Exchange of Winnings form a bridge between the two major structural elements of
the poem by suggesting the exchange of blows between Bercilak
and Gawain and by climaxing each day's temptation, but it also
foreshadows and motivates the final testing of Gawain by Bercilak
at the Green Chapel.

Kittredge also listed as elements which were "certainly added
or greatly elaborated by the English author":

the learned introductory stanza summarizing the fabulous settlements
of Western Europe . . . ; the description of the Christmas festivities
(i, 3) and that of the Green Knight (i, 7–9); the challenge (i, 12–13)
and the speech of Gawain (i, 16); the highly poetical stanzas on the
changing seasons (ii, 1–2); the very elaborate description of the process
of arming a knight (ii, 4–6), with the allegorical account of the pentangle of virtues (ii, 7); Gawain's itinerary—Logres, North Wales,
Anglesea, Holyhead, the wilderness of Wirral (ii, 9); the winter piece
(ii, 10); the justly celebrated account of the three hunts (ii, 1 ff.).[38]

In these added elements, certainly, the real greatness of the poem lies. For no matter what he may believe about the origins of the plot and characters, it is to these sections of the poem added by the English poet that the reader finds himself drawn. The initial clash of Bercilak and Gawain, the lovely passage on the changing seasons, Gawain's wild journey to the North, the hunts—these are the great literary passages; and in these the original genius of the poet, as well as his most conspicuous use of the medieval literary traditions, is most apparent.

By the inclusion of fresh, imaginative detail, the Green Knight is made a figure of genuine terror, not a stylized bogeyman out of an Irish fairy tale; and the description of Gawain's journey through the frozen Wirral forest demonstrates clearly the poet's habit, observable throughout his work, of seeing with fresh eyes and with a marvelous sense of detail scenes usually presented in medieval literature as general, unrealized tableaux:

> With sleet nearly slain,   he slept in his armor
> More nights than enough   on the naked rocks,
> Where splashing the cold stream   sprang from the summit,
> And hung in hard icicles   high o'er his head.   (729–32)

Nearly all the commentators have singled out this use of detail as the poet's most accomplished poetic technique. The extraordinary visual effectiveness of the poems is accomplished not only by the poet's singular ability in the descriptive scenes to select and concentrate on those details which best typify the mood and character of the scene—Gawain's sleeping on rocks in his armor, for example, during his journey through the Wirral—but also by his habit of adopting "the point of view of the characters central in a given narrative passage as that character responds to the circumstances of the action. The result is vividness . . . of a special kind. When it is visual, it depends as much on the exact appropriateness of what is seen, by whom, and from where, as on the color, texture, or other intrinsic sensory or aesthetic qualities of the object." [39]

The sharply detailed scenes in Bercilak's court and especially the interviews between Gawain and Bercilak's lady, for example, bring home to the reader, as do no other passages in medieval literature, a full and living sense of the meaning of *gentilesse*, the chivalric code of manners. Not even in Chaucer's *Troilus and*

Criseyde does one find the inmost quality of courtly manners and attitudes so perfectly translated into dramatic terms. All too often chivalry is regarded as a literary pose, as an artificial, codified set of manners existing only in the courtesy books and in the stylized romances of the period. In *Sir Gawain and the Green Knight* the reader everywhere feels—and this is due entirely to the art of the poet, to his ability to enter into his characters—that he is not observing literary mannequins, but people whose grace and wit are parts of a cultivated and operative system of manners that governs their conduct and imparts to their lives a dignity and charm that is, like the elegance of their costume, sharply at odds with the terrifyingly brutal world beyond their castles.

VI *Myth*

Sir Gawain and the Green Knight in its balanced and coherent structure, its skillful adaptation and functional use of its sources and traditional elements, its original use of meter and language, and its sharply-defined scenes of courtly life reveals, in the same way as did his earlier poems but in much fuller measure, the superlative talent of the *Pearl*-poet. And the poem makes it clear also that the poet's talent as it developed constantly sought after new forms of expression. In *Patience* and *Purity,* the poet used familiar biblical narratives as vehicles; in *Pearl* he turned to the elegiac and to the dream-vision conventions. *Sir Gawain and the Green Knight* is a courtly romance whose narrative and descriptive elements reach far back into Celtic myth.

Nor does this variety in source material in the four poems represent experimentation for its own sake. As we have seen, one of the distinctive marks of the *Pearl*-poet's method and talent has been his ability to use, albeit sometimes in a highly original fashion, the basic elements of his sources for thematic purposes. The Jonah story as seen by the *Pearl*-poet is a parable of disobedience; the Old Testament narratives in *Purity* contain in themselves the seeds of the interpretation given to them by the poet; the elegiac and dream-vision traditions form a perfect medium for the themes of *Pearl.*

A number of critics have attempted to find a key to the theme of the poem in the myths so carefully joined by the poet to make up the narrative structure of *Sir Gawain and the Green Knight.*

And certainly, no matter what we may think of the actual mythical interpretations of the poem that have been brought forward, it has become increasingly clear that the myths involved in the poem do to a large extent determine its ultimate meaning. We have seen already how in many cases this question of the *use* of myth in the poem—that is, the way in which the folk sources which make up the structure of the poem have been transmitted and joined—has frequently, as in the attempts to isolate and trace Celtic elements, touched upon the *meaning* of those same myths in the poem.

In general, however, these early myth-hunting critics were concerned only with the relationship of the folk elements in *Sir Gawain and the Green Knight* and not at all with the structures of meaning which these myths carried in themselves and hence contributed to the total meaning of the poem. Only with the rise of "myth criticism" in the 1940s and 1950s did such issues begin to occupy the attention of scholars and critics generally; and it was inevitable that *Sir Gawain and the Green Knight*, in which the origins of the mythic sources of the poem had already been thoroughly classified and traced, should become a prime subject for investigation.

The greatest single impetus to the investigation of myth in the poem came from a now-famous article by the English critic John Speirs in 1949, the basic premise of which we have already quoted in connection with the use by the poet of various Celtic elements.[40] Roughly following the vegetation myth theory of origin already laid down by E. K. Chambers, A. B. Cook, and W. A. Nitze,[41] Speirs argued that the poem was a "midwinter festival poem" in which "Gawain is seen in his traditional role as the hero, the agent who brought back the spring, restored the frozen life-processes, revived the god—or (in later versions) cured the king."[42]

The importance of Speirs's article, however, lay not so much in its conclusions, which had already been suggested by other critics, but in its brash assertion that all previous attempts to trace the origins of the poem in Celtic tradition and French romance, in fact all investigative scholarship devoted to the poem, had been worthless or, worse still, misleading. The *only* way of approach to the poem, asserted Speirs, was through its "inner organizing, unifying and realizing principle of life and growth."[43] As one commentator has remarked, Speirs's "position is argued with such vigor and dogmatism that he has given new life to *Gawain* scholarship." [44]

As might be expected, most scholars writing on the poem since 1949 do not share Speirs's thesis, not so much because of his specific conclusions about the poem which were, as we have said, not startlingly original, but because of his underlying assumption that the poem does not merely reflect the mythic or ritual elements inherent in the sources, but that these myths and rituals are consciously invoked by the poet in order to contribute to the meaning of the poem. Thus Speirs's article, despite its great interest, has proved after all to be a false scent, for, although scholars have continued to investigate the mythic and folklore sources of the poem, they have not generally accepted Speirs's assertion that the poet's use of myth is conscious nor have they followed his general identification of myth and poem. Instead, these scholars have concentrated, as did the older generation of scholars, on the specific ways in which the mythic elements determine the structure and meaning of the poem. [45]

For example, the mythic Morgan le Fay is surely the most controversial figure in the poem, and her ambiguous role has become the crux of the poem for a number of critics. It is of course puzzling that, although Morgan appears in the poem only once and is named only twice, with her influence on the action discussed in a single passage of but twenty-one lines, she is said by the poet to be the prime mover of the entire action. Certainly critical opinion has been divided on the role that Morgan plays in the poem. Kittredge, writing in 1916, asserted that Morgan's action stemmed from her traditional hatred of Guinevere and from a desire to warn the court of the queen's unfaithfulness; he concluded that the poet had through his use of Morgan supplied the medieval reader familiar with her general role in the Arthur legend with an entirely adequate explanation of Bercilak's motives. [46] J. R. Hulbert, however, writing in the same year, saw Bercilak's explanation as "inherently unreasonable" and condemned it as a last-minute attempt by the poet to supply Bercilak with some sort of explanation for his actions. [47]

More modern criticism has come no closer to agreement. While one critic has suggested that Morgan intended to purge Arthur's court of moral depravity and that her plan did in fact succeed in humiliating Arthur,[48] another has answered his argument point by point and has asserted that Morgan is present in the poem "solely as a foil to enhance the beauty of Gawain's temptress." [49]

Mother Angela Carson has stated that Morgan le Fay, who is traditionally a shape-shifter, actually appears in the poem both as the old woman whom Gawain sees in Bercilak's chapel and also as Bercilak's fair wife.[50] Mother Carson also asserts that Morgan's dual role would have been perfectly obvious to a medieval audience acquainted with her traditional roles as witch and temptress. Bercilak thus would have been readily identified by the poet's audience with Urien, traditionally Morgan's lover, who is also sometimes said to be a king of the Celtic Other World, that mysterious realm entered only occasionally and at great risk by mortals. Much of Mother Carson's argument deals with the journey of Gawain, which she identifies with the chivalric quest for the Other World, complete with the usual water barriers and fairy mounds. Morgan herself appears in the poem in a number of her traditional roles—as shape-shifter, seductress, enemy of Arthur and Guinevere, ugly old woman, beautiful fay—all of which would have been readily recognizable by the poet's audience and would have contributed to the significance of Bercilak's statement that she is the sole motivator of the action.

And perhaps the answer to the puzzling question of Morgan's influence on the action does indeed lie in her traditional character. For, even though Friedman and Mother Carson reject the idea, the tradition of Morgan le Fay does include her role as healer and tester; and it is perfectly in character, as Kittredge and Denver Baughan have demonstrated, for her to test the honor, fidelity, and morality of individuals. That the poem does involve testing, no critic has doubted; and, although the precise qualities being tested have been debated, courage, fidelity, and chastity are certainly among them.

VII *Morality*

The testing of Gawain involves a strong ethical and moral element, but critics are divided as to the degree of success with which Gawain meets his test. One critic, for example, maintains that Gawain, in spite of his apparent failure to keep faith with Bercilak, is nevertheless a "splendid man" and that his actions demonstrate "what a perfect knight can do when he is forced to face the unknown." [51] Yet another critic maintains that the poem is concerned with the irony of Gawain's "muddled conscience," [52] and still another holds that the poem is "a human and sympathetic presentation designed to reveal how human and imperfect is even a supposedly perfect knight such as the pentagonal Gawain." [53] And various studies of the poem's several confession scenes,[54] of the penitential doctrines reflected in the poem,[55] and of the imagery of the Grail quest underlying the poem[56] have emphasized the ethical and, specifically, the Christian nature of *Sir Gawain and the Green Knight.*

However, the success of Gawain's conduct under fire can only rightly be judged in terms of the total ordeal which he undergoes, a test that involves not only his treatment at the hands of the Green Knight and Bercilak's lady, but the entire journey which he is forced to undertake as a result of his acceptance of the Green Knight's challenge. For Gawain's entire journey is described by the poet in terms which mark it as moral and spiritual rather than as merely chivalric. The usual quest of the romances is, of course, undertaken in response to a challenge superficially very like that of the Green Knight—a maiden's plea for help against enchantment or the mysterious appearance of a stag; but, aside from the quest of the Holy Grail, the resulting journey consists of adventures designed to test, if they test anything at all, the prowess and courage of the hero, not his morality. However, the quest of Gawain for the Green Knight is from its very beginning shown to be of a different sort, involving as it does not only prowess and courage, but also chastity and loyalty. Whether or not one agrees with Professor Denver Baughan's assertion that Arthur, because of his pride, is unable to strike even a single blow with the Green Knight's ax and can do no more than flail it about ineffectively,[57] it is clear that only Gawain among all Arthur's knights can qualify for the adventure by beheading the Green Knight, and that he, the best of the knights, goes forth to be tested as a representative of the Round Table civilization.

The imagery of the quest supports this conception of the moral nature of Gawain's quest. The pentangle on his shield symbolizes the religious virtues which he embodies, and an image of the Blessed Virgin adorns the inner side of the shield. He prays to the Blessed Virgin for relief on his journey (737–39) and is said to be

under her special protection (1769). The forests through which
he passes are filled with wild beasts and with savages who love
neither God nor their fellow men (702). He discovers Bercilak's
castle immediately upon praying for "some lodging wherein to
hear mass" (755). Gawain himself, moreover, recognizes that he
is attempting the quest in obedience to God's will (2156 ff., 2208
ff.) and that his fate is in the hands of God (1967, 2136 ff.).[58]

The effect of this quest is, first of all, to force Gawain to con-
front the violence and terror of the world outside Arthur's warm,
complacent court. At least two commentators have seen in this
contrast of civilized court and grim, untamed forest the principal
theme of the poem: the "idea that the primitive and sometimes
brutal forces of nature make known their demands to all men,
even to those who would take shelter behind the civilized comforts of court life." [59]

Second, the quest serves to introduce Gawain to a court which
may very well be superior in grace to that of Arthur; certainly, at
moments of crisis its members challenge the ability of the Round
Table and of its best knight, Gawain, to meet the demands made
upon it. When the knights of the Round Table cringe before him,
the Green Knight says:

> "What!" quoth the hero,   "Is this Arthur's household,
> The fame of whose fellowship   fills many kingdoms?
> Now where is your vainglory?   Where are your victories?
> Where is your grimness,   your great words, your anger?"
> (308–11)

Again, when Gawain resists the advances of Bercilak's lady, she is
amazed that the famous Gawain could be ignorant of proper
courtly etiquette:

> He who blesses all words   reward this reception!
> I doubt if indeed   I may dub you Gawain.
>
> .   .   .   .
>
> One as good as is Gawain   the gracious considered,
> (And courtly behavior's   found wholly in him)
> Not lightly so long   could remain with a lady
> Without, in courtesy,   craving a kiss
> At some slight subtle hint   at the end of a story.
> (1291–2, 1296–1300)

Finally, when Gawain evades his first stroke, the Green Knight says:

> Not Gawain thou art   who so good is considered,
> Ne'er daunted by host   in hill or in dale;
> Now in fear, ere thou feelest   a hurt, thou art flinching;
> Such cowardice never   I knew of that knight.   (2270–73)

Thus the Green Knight and his lady find the chivalry of the Round Table lacking in the fundamentals of courage and courtesy. And although the exact motives of Morgan le Fay seem to us, if not to the poet's audience, obscure, we had best take Bercilak, who should know, at his word when he announces that he was sent to "test the pride" of Arthur's court. It seems reasonably clear also that Gawain, in spite of his prowess and integrity, fails at least that part of the test which involves the keeping of faith. In the end, the temptation to save his own life, even at the expense of breaking his word to Bercilak, manages to overcome even Gawain's most sacred chivalric vows; and he returns home, the poem makes clear, overwhelmed by shame. Critic Alan Markman may feel that Gawain is a "splendid man," but Gawain certainly does not.

In Gawain's failure, then, lies that of the court and of the whole Round Table society. Morgan le Fay, whatever her intentions, has failed since Guinevere is still alive and since the court, far from humiliated by Gawain's failure, laughingly transforms the knight's girdle, which he regards as a badge of shame, into a baldric of honor. Whether or not the poet intended the court's failure to recognize the implications of Gawain's test—that they themselves would have fared far worse than did Gawain and so are more prone than he to failure—to stand as a foreshadowing of the final decay and destruction of Arthur's civilization cannot with any certainty be proved, although this might be the case. At any rate, the poem gains immeasurably in what Matthew Arnold called "high seriousness" when the presence of Morgan le Fay is seen as integral to the poem and when the failure of Gawain is recognized.

Yet, in spite of its obviously ethical and moral nature, the poem is a gay and happy affair. Certainly the "vividness of the language, the subtleties of the lines, the extraordinary lightness of tone, all bespeak a sophistication and irony, a sense of humor, which illuminates the whole thing from beginning to end." [60] And surely the comic elements of the poem—its extravagance in description and conversation, for example—are necessary to the balance of feelings which in this poem, as in *Pearl*, serves to avoid any taint of either bathos or sentimentality. As Robert Penn Warren pointed out in regard to the balcony scene in *Romeo and Juliet*, the "effect might even be more vulnerable poetically if the impurities were purged away." [61] We are faced with a poem which does obviously have room for "impurities" of tone, for both "bliss and care"; and the "impurities" of comedy thus serve to temper Gawain's failure, though oddly enough also to make it human and understandable.

The foregoing account of the major areas of interest in the poem should reveal the principal barrier to any clear statement of the poem's central theme: the complexity of tone, idea, and form which the poem everywhere reveals. In the end it is well-nigh impossible to say with any degree of assurance *exactly* what *Sir Gawain and the Green Knight* is *only* about. The poem is certainly about society, both flourishing and decadent; but it involves not only the relationship between civilization and nature and the responsibility of the individual to society, but also the individual's responsibility to himself—to his own deals of conduct and, ultimately, to his survival.

The poet's thoughts on these matters are complex; the poem is no simple rule book, but a rich and varied commentary on life. As we have seen, Gawain is in his own eyes a failure, but in the eyes of his society he is an enormous success. Within the castle all is gaiety and warmth, yet outside horrible beasts and icy storms and godless men await even the best of knights on the most godly of errands. Bercilak's lady is lovely and charming, yet she is wanton and in the end lures Gawain into disgrace. Bercilak is both monster and courtier. And we could go on for some time listing such paradoxes as these from the poem without really coming any closer to the point.

Nor does further investigation of the traditions that make up the poem really settle the issue. The poem is a romance, to be sure, and, like the romances that precede it, contains certain more-or-less standard characteristics: feasts, hunts, tourneys, descriptions of arms, lonely quests, hairbreadth escapes, supernatural monsters—the lot. Yet *Sir Gawain and the Green Knight* is obviously no ordinary romance, and an analysis of the ways in which the poem conforms to its type leads only to the conclusion that its essence is not here.

Much the same point can be made about the use of courtly love in the poem. For, although the heyday of courtly love as a way of life (if, indeed, it ever were) was long since past by the time of the *Pearl*-poet, its influence is certainly to be seen in the poem. The lady obviously either is or pretends to be a devotee of *fin amor*, though an unusually aggressive one; and she is disappointed at Gawain's unwillingness to play the game. Yet while courtly love is presented as a snare and a temptation, Gawain successfully resists its lures, and it is clear that courtly love is only a part of the poem's interplay of theme and idea, not its core.

In short, no single approach to the poem can ever illuminate all of its many facets. The scores of studies of sources, symbols, poetic devices, and literary traditions have served to remove some of the shadows which time has cast over the poem, and no one can doubt that future studies will clarify much that is now obscure and dark. But no matter how pointed and well-directed, such studies can never reduce to a single set of literary or moral principles the tangled web of Gawain's search for knightly perfection. For by means of its dramatization of the complexity of human motives and in its willingness to see human conduct and morality as in the end irreducible to precepts and formulas, *Sir Gawain and the Green Knight* itself becomes as deep almost as life and a lasting image of our humanity.

CHAPTER 6

Conclusion

I T is a difficult matter to write a summary of a summary, and the first five chapters of this volume have been in fact summary in that they have merely touched upon the central issues concerning the *Pearl*-poet. The tremendous amount of work devoted to *Pearl* and to *Sir Gawain and the Green Knight* reported in these pages should indicate not only that the poems of the *Pearl*-poet are very much alive today but that the scholarship devoted to these poems will probably increase. For the astonishing thing is that there is still so much to do. *Patience* and *Purity*, for example, have been left virtually untouched; it is a source of amazement to me that, aside from a few purely linguistic studies, not one serious work on *Purity* has ever been published. And even though *Pearl* and *Sir Gawain and the Green Knight* have certainly been approached from almost every conceivable angle, there still remain areas of these poems to be explored.

Our greatest need, however, seems now to be for studies in which the works of the *Pearl*-poet are taken as a whole. Such studies need not and should not be largely biographical, cultural, or linguistic; they should be devoted to establishing the central themes and techniques of the poet, to demonstrating not only the mechanical unity of the poems, but also their organic unity, which is the poet's vision of life.

One great help to such studies, now unavailable, would be a complete, unified edition of Cotton Nero A.x. At present there are in print excellent editions of *Pearl* and of *Sir Gawain and the Green Knight*, but Bateson's edition of *Patience* and Menner's of *Purity* are very difficult to obtain. This single working-edition of the four poems should be edited according to a single policy and should incorporate certain features that would vastly aid comparative scholarship—a unified glossary, which would in fact be a concordance; a thorough set of notes reflecting all the available scholarship; and a comparison of the various linguistic forms found throughout the manuscript.

Even though such an edition and such studies of the whole poet are now unavailable, some generalizations and prognostications are possible. First, it should be clear that the four poems of Cotton Nero A.x. are by the same author. Language, meter, habits of composition, organization, themes, images—all of these point toward unity of authorship. Once this premise is accepted, the critic can cease begging the fruitless question of common authorship and begin to draw from each of the four poems the subtle echoes of the others in language, style, and imagery that establish the patterns of theme and idea common to all.

Second, we can certainly establish the fact that in any consideration of the whole poet, *Patience* and *Purity* are of great importance. True, these poems will never be anthologized as are *Pearl* and, especially, *Sir Gawain and the Green Knight*. But then neither are *Troilus and Cressida* and *Coriolanus* greatly anthologized, though no one would deny their importance to the study of Shakespeare. And not only are *Patience* and *Purity* of great importance in isolating and evaluating certain techniques and themes in the later poems, but they are worth investigation in their own right.

Third, we should be able to assert without question the sheer technical genius of the poet, and we should be prepared to study further his creative use of the traditions of verse and language open to him. The four poems of Cotton Nero A.x. exhibit a steady increase not only in metrical and rhetorical skill, but also in sheer technical exuberance, in the joy of creating new and subtle variations in old patterns. The more we find out about the kind of language and the kind of style used by the poet, the closer we can come to establishing something of his intentions.

Fourth, it should be apparent even now that the *Pearl*-poet is essentially a moral poet and that any attempt to understand the unity of his work will have to begin and end with the ethical and theological nature of the poems. It would be profitless, I think, to approach the poet, however thoroughly and with however good intentions, simply as an entertainer, as a cultural historian, or as an artist in any restricted modern use of that term. For this poet clearly has something to say about the conduct of life. As we have seen, *Purity, Pearl,* and *Sir Gawain and the Green Knight* all deal with the relation of sexual morality and loyalty to one's code of conduct, both secular and religious. And *Patience,* though it does not deal with sexual purity, is certainly linked to the other three poems through its concern with obedience to God's commandments.

Purity presents these two themes by the use of contrasting and, at times, overlapping biblical stories of impurity and unfaithfulness; *Pearl* contrasts the purity and obedience of the pearl-maiden with the restless "grouching" (a theme first developed in *Patience*) of the narrator-father; Sir Gawain is tested both for sexual purity and for obedience to his word. In all three cases, the qualities of purity and obedience are closely related: failure in obedience to God, as seen in the Hebrews in *Purity,* leads to impurity and sacrilege; the spotless innocence of the pearl-maiden, on the other hand, seems almost to symbolize her unquestioning obedience to God's will, just as her father's inability to accept what seems to him the arbitrary nature of God's disposition of the saved souls in Heaven reflects his essential worldliness; and Gawain, although he passes Morgan's test for sexual purity, ultimately fails in resisting the temptation to save his life, even though saving it results in his breaking his given word.

All four poems thus involve failures in purity and/or obedience, and the difference between success and failure is generally treated by the poet in specifically Christian terms. The disobedience of Jonah and the ancient Hebrews in *Purity* is directly opposed to the commands of Jehovah. The grumbling failure of the narrator in *Pearl* to accept God's judgment is directly contrary to the will of God as stated by the maiden. And, in *Sir Gawain and the Green Knight,* Gawain fails in being obedient to his word in spite of the symbolic protection of his armor with its pentangle of Christian virtues and the personal guidance of the Blessed Virgin. The pure and constant values of Heaven are, therefore, contrasted in all four poems with the tarnished and shifting standards of earth.

What these instances of religious failure lead to is a general vision of Man in the *Pearl*-poet as fallen, degenerate, and incapable in himself of achieving salvation, of attaining true felicity, or even of maintaining a decent standard of conduct in life. The poet consistently sees society as corrupt; even the civilization of Arthur, that golden, chivalric court in its "first age," is essentially cowardly and frivolous. The man who wishes to live by God's standards is thus presented as being constantly in conflict with the values of society; his greatest temptation is to take the easy road away from the strictures of God. And the *Pearl*-poet is unyielding on this point: to accept God's appointed mission is to bring upon oneself the scorn and fury of the world. Jonah, the Old Testament heroes in *Purity*, the father in *Pearl*, and Sir Gawain do not avoid present trouble—though they may, as in *Purity*, escape eternal damnation —by taking up their crosses to follow God. Jonah is far happier sleeping on the ship, falsely certain that he has escaped God, than he ever is preaching God's word; the father's discovery of the pearl-maiden's glorification in Heaven brings him only confusion and unhappiness; Gawain would have, in a sense, been far better off at home in Arthur's gay court than lost in the frozen Wirral, attacked by outlaws and terrifying beasts.

Yet society in these poems—unless, like the Ninevites in *Patience*, it turns to God—is doomed, even as the Round Table is, by its own inherent, fallen sinfulness; only a handful of heroes, set upon and despised, can hope for the mercy of God and for salvation in the orthodox Christian way, through the merits of Christ. Thus the father of the pearl-maiden and Gawain have in the end attained a measure of wisdom, though they are overcome by a sense of their own unworthiness and by a perception of the wrongness of the world in which they live. While I am perhaps guilty of describing the *Pearl*-poet in terms more applicable to T. S. Eliot or to Graham Greene than to a medieval clerk, yet I do not think these comparisons inappropriate. All these writers are parts of the same Catholic tradition and share essentially the same moral vision of Man struggling for grace in a fallen world.

Nevertheless, in making such comparisons we must always hold before us an image of the uniqueness of the *Pearl*-poet. That he is to some degree the product of his age is, of course, undeniable; yet, like Shakespeare, he is most importantly for all time. That he was influenced by others—by older poets of the alliterative tradition, by the contemporary French and London poets, by teachers, and perhaps even by his secular masters—is true; but thousands of his contemporaries were subject to the same influences and there is still only one *Sir Gawain and the Green Knight*. We can be relatively sure that he in turn influenced countless poets, yet we see him best in his own poems and not as he appears in the works of others. We must thus work carefully to establish and then to preserve the essence and the integrity of this poet who, next to Chaucer, is our greatest heritage from the fourteenth century.

Notes and References

PREFACE

1. E. Talbot Donaldson, "Patristic Exegesis in the Criticism of Medieval Literature: The Opposition," in *Critical Approaches to Medieval Literature: Selected Papers from the English Institute 1958–1959,* ed. Dorothy Bethurum (New York, 1960), p. 1.

2. Robert E. Kaske, "The *Canticum Canticorum* in the *Miller's Tale,*" *Studies in Philology,* LIX (1962), 479–500.

3. D. W. Robertson, Jr., *A Preface to Chaucer: Studies in Medieval Perspectives* (Princeton, 1962), p. 48.

4. See Larry D. Benson, "The Authorship of St. Erkenwald," *Journal of English and Germanic Philology,* LXIV (1965), 393–405.

CHAPTER ONE

1. See J. R. Hulbert, "A Hypothesis Concerning the Alliterative Revival," *Modern Philology,* XXVIII (1931), 405–22.

2. *The Awntyrs of Arthure,* ll. 62–3.

3. *Piers Plowman,* C-text, XVIII, 289–91.

4. *Wynnere and Wastoure,* ll. 230 ff.

5. C. S. Lewis, *The Allegory of Love* (London, 1936), p. 12.

6. *Ibid.,* pp. 6 ff.

7. *Sir Gawain and the Green Knight,* ll. 740 ff. The translation is that of Theodore Howard Banks, Jr. (New York, 1929).

8. In *Medieval English Poetry: The Non-Chaucerian Tradition* (London, 1957).

9. The title "clerk" in the Middle Ages was used to refer to a man who had taken "minor" (as opposed to "holy") orders in the Church and hence could read, write, and perform certain subordinate ecclesiastical duties. Clerks could thus be put to various uses in noble households where there were many records to be kept and, quite usually, many prayers to be said.

10. Henry L. Savage, *The Gawain-Poet: Studies in His Personality and Background* (Chapel Hill, 1956).

11. Particularly, among others, by George Neilson in *Huchown of the Awle Ryale, the Alliterative Poet* (Glasgow, 1902).

12. Oscar Cargill and Margaret Schlauch, "*The Pearl* and Its Jeweller," *PMLA*, XLIII (1928), 105–23.

13. C. O. Chapman, "The Authorship of the *Pearl*," *PMLA*, XLVII (1932), 346–53.

14. J. P. Oakden, *Alliterative Poetry in Middle English* (Manchester, 1930–35), I, 257–61.

15. Sir Israel Gollancz in *The Cambridge History of English Literature*. Interestingly enough, Gollancz may well have inadvertently combined a Ralph Strode mentioned in a list of the Fellows of Merton College, Oxford, in 1360 with the Ralph Strode traditionally spoken of as a poet *and* with a London lawyer of the same name to produce a wholly fictional fourteenth-century figure (See Carleton F. Brown, "Note on the Question of Strode's Authorship of *The Pearl*," *PMLA*, XIX [1904], 146–48).

16. See C. O. Chapman, "Virgil and the *Gawain*-Poet," *PMLA*, LX (1945), 16–23; C. O. Chapman, "Chaucer and the *Gawain*-Poet: A Conjecture," *Modern Language Notes*, LXVIII (1953), 521–24.

17. Walter Kirkland Greene, "The *Pearl*: A New Interpretation," *PMLA*, XL (1925), 814–27.

18. Savage, p. 10.

19. Carleton F. Brown, "The Author of *The Pearl* Considered in the Light of his Theological Opinions," *PMLA*, XIX (1904), 115–45.

20. Savage, pp. 20–21, and Dorothy Everett and Naomi D. Hurnard, "Legal Phraseology in a Passage in *Pearl*," *Medium Aevum*, XVI (1947), 9–15.

21. E. Wintermute, "The *Pearl's* Author as Herbalist," *Modern Language Notes*, LXIV (1949), 83–4.

22. C. O. Chapman, "The Musical Training of the *Pearl* Poet," *PMLA*, XLVI (1931), 177–81.

23. Savage, pp. 21 ff.

24. *Ibid.*, p. 16.

25. *Sir Gawain and the Green Knight*, ll. 2171 ff.

26. *The Pearl*, ll. 41 ff. The translation is that of Sophie Jewett (New York, 1908).

27. Particularly Gollancz in *The Cambridge History of English Literature*, I, 133 ff.

28. See Robert Menner (ed.), *Purity, A Middle English Poem* (New Haven, 1920), pp. xxx-xxxvii, for a detailed analysis of the order of the poems.

29. John W. Clark in "The *Gawain*-Poet and the Substantival Adjective," *Journal of English and Germanic Philology*, XLIX (1950), 60–66; "Observations on Certain Differences in Vocabulary between *Cleanness* and *Sir Gawain and the Green Knight*," *Philological Quarterly*, XXVIII (1949), 261–73; "Paraphrases for 'God' in the Poems

Attributed to 'The *Gawain*-Poet,'" *Modern Language Notes,* LXV (1950), 232–36; "On Certain 'Alliterative' and 'Poetic' Words in the Poems Attributed to 'The *Gawain*-Poet,'" *Modern Language Quarterly,* XII (1951), 387–98.

30. John Dale Ebbs, "Stylistic Mannerisms of the *Gawain-Poet,*" *Journal of English and Germanic Philology,* LVII (1958), 522–25.

31. Menner, pp. xvii–xviii.

32. *Ibid.,* p. xvi.

33. *Ibid.,* pp. xii and 67–8.

34. *Ibid.,* p. xiv.

35. E. V. Gordon (ed.), *Pearl* (London, 1953), p. xliv.

36. *Patience,* ll. 2–3.

37. *Pearl,* ll. 1189 ff.

38. Gordon, *Pearl,* p. xliii.

39. J. R. R. Tolkien and E. V. Gordon (eds.), *Sir Gawain and the Green Knight* (Oxford, 1946), p. xx.

40. Savage, p. 6.

41. Menner, p. xxix.

42. See Gordon, *Pearl,* p. xliv, n. 2.

43. M. S. Serjeantson, "The Dialects of the West Midlands in Middle English," *Review of English Studies,* III (1927), 327.

44. G. P. J., "The Author of *Sir Gawain and the Green Knight,*" *Notes and Queries,* n.s. III (1956), 53–54.

CHAPTER TWO

1. In *Early English Alliterative Poems,* Early English Text Society, Original Series I (London, 1864), p. xi.

2. Following Menner's evidence (*Purity, A Middle English Poem* [New Haven, 1920], pp. xxx–xxxviii), I would place it third, after *Patience* and *Purity* and before *Sir Gawain and the Green Knight.*

3. *The Pearl,* ll. 5–6. The translation quoted, which is for the most part quite loose, is that of Sophie Jewett (New York, 1908). A few translations of phrases are my own. The most recent, and best, edition of the Middle English text is that of E. V. Gordon (London, 1953).

4. George T. Wright, *The Poet in the Poem: The Personae of Eliot, Yeats, and Pound* (Berkeley, 1960).

5. *The Works of Plato,* ed. B. Jowett, Vol. II: *The Republic* (New York, n.d.), p. 479.

6. *The Poetics,* tr. W. H. Fyfe (Cambridge, Mass., 1953), pp. 97 ff.

7. In a recent article ("Chaucer's Self-Portrait in *The Book of the Duchess,*" *Philological Quarterly,* XLIII [1964], 27–39), J. Burke Severs asserts that Chaucer did in fact wish his audience to make an identification.

8. Francis Fergusson, *Dante's Drama of the Mind: A Modern Reading of the Purgatorio* (Princeton, 1953), p. 10.

9. *Ibid.*, p. 9.

10. R. W. Chambers, Preface to *New Light on 'Piers Plowman'* by Allan H. Bright (London, 1950), p. 19.

11. *Pearl*, ed. Gordon, p. xv.

12. A view also maintained by Gordon; C. G. Osgood (*The Pearl: A Middle-English Poem* [Boston, 1906]); I. Gollancz (*Cambridge History of English Literature*, I, 357–61); René Wellek ("*The Pearl:* An Interpretation of the Middle English Poem," Charles University *Studies in English*, IV [1933], 1–33); Dorothy Everett (*Essays on Middle English Literature* [London, 1955]); and S. de V. Hoffman ("The *Pearl:* Notes for an Interpretation," *Modern Philology*, LVIII [1960], 73–80).

13. W. H. Schofield, "The Nature and Fabric of The *Pearl*," *PMLA*, XIX (1904), 154–215, and "Symbolism, Allegory, and Autobiography in The *Pearl*," *PMLA*, XXIV (1909), 585–675.

14. G. G. Coulton, "In Defence of 'Pearl'," *Modern Language Review*, II (1906), 39–43.

15. R. M. Garrett, "*The Pearl:* An Interpretation," University of Washington *Studies in English*, IV (1918), 1–48.

16. J. B. Fletcher, "The Allegory of The *Pearl*," *Journal of English and Germanic Philology*, XX (1921), 1–21.

17. Sister Mary Madeleva, *Pearl: A Study in Spiritual Dryness* (New York, 1925).

18. W. K. Greene, "*The Pearl:* A New Interpretation," *PMLA*, XL (1925), 814–27.

19. Sister Mary Vincent Hillmann, "Some Debatable Words in *Pearl* and its Theme," *Modern Language Notes*, LX (1945), 241–48.

20. Bruno McAndrew, "*The Pearl*, A Catholic *Paradise Lost*," *American Benedictine Review*, VIII (1957), 243–51.

21. Wendell Stacy Johnson, "The Imagery and Diction of The *Pearl:* Toward an Interpretation," *ELH*, XX (1953), 161–80.

22. Marie Padgett Hamilton. "The Meaning of the Middle English *Pearl*," *PMLA*, LXX (1955), 805–24.

23. *The Basic Writings of St. Thomas Aquinas*, ed. Anton C. Pegis, Vol. I: *Summa Theologica* (New York, 1945), Q. I, Art. 10, pp. 16–17.

24. D. W. Robertson, "The Pearl as a Symbol," *Modern Language Notes*, LXV (1950), 155–61.

25. Milton R. Stern, "An Approach to The Pearl," *Journal of English and Germanic Philology*, LIV (1955), 684–92.

26. The value of the multi-level approach in the study of secular literature has been effectively questioned by R. H. Green ("Dante's 'Allegory of Poets' and the Medieval Theory of Poetic Fiction," *Com-*

parative Literature, IX [1957], 118–28); M. W. Bloomfield ("Symbolism in Medieval Literature," *Modern Philology*, LVI [1958], 73–81); E. Talbot Donaldson ("Patristic Exegesis in the Criticism of Medieval Literature: The Opposition" in *Critical Approaches to Medieval Literature: Selected Papers from the English Institute* 1958–1959, ed. Dorothy Bethurum [New York, 1960], pp. 1–26); and by S. de V. Hoffman (*op. cit.*).

27. Robert E. Kaske, "Patristic Exegesis: The Defense" in *Critical Approaches to Medieval Literature*, p. 30.

28. In the dedicatory epistle ("Epistola X") to the "Paradiso" addressed to Dante's patron, Can Grande della Scala.

29. *Pearl*, ed. Gordon, p. xii.

30. Notably Wendell Stacy Johnson; C. O. Chapman ("The Musical Training of the *Pearl* Poet," *PMLA*, XLVI [1931], 177–81, and "Numerical Symbolism in Dante and the *Pearl*," *Modern Language Notes*, LIV [1939], 256–59); John Speirs (*Medieval English Poetry: The Non-Chaucerian Tradition* [London, 1957]); Edwin Wintermute ("The *Pearl's* Author as Herbalist," *Modern Language Notes*, LXIV [1949], 83–4); Edwin Dodge Cuffe, S. J. ("An Interpretation of *Patience, Cleanness*, and *The Pearl* from the Viewpoint of Imagery," unpublished Ph.D. dissertation, University of North Carolina, 1951); R. W. V. Elliott ("*Pearl* and the Medieval Garden: Convention or Originality?" *Langues Modernes*, XIV [1951]); Dorothy Everett and Naomi D. Hurnard ("Legal Phraseology in a Passage in *Pearl*," *Medium Aevum*, XVI [1947], 9–15); P. Heather ("Precious Stones in the Middle English Verse of the Fourteenth Century," *Folklore*, XLII [1931], 217–264, 345–404); William J. Knightly ("Pearl: 'the Hy seysoun,'" *Modern Language Notes*, LXXVI [1961], 97–102); and Ian Bishop, "The Significance of the 'Garlande Gay' in the Allegory of 'Pearl,'" *Review of English Studies*, VIII [1957], 12–21).

31. Cuffe, p. 209.

32. See especially A. C. Spearing ("Symbolic and Dramatic Development in *Pearl*," *Modern Philology*, LX [1962], 1–12) for a discussion of the development of the symbol of the pearl within the poem.

33. See C. A. Luttrell, "The Medieval Tradition of the Pearl Virginity," *Medium Aevum*, XXXI (1962), 194–200.

34. C. F. Brown, "The Author of *The Pearl*, Considered in the Light of His Theological Opinions," *PMLA*, XIX (1904), 115–45.

35. For discussions of this and related questions see Marie Padgett Hamilton ("The Orthodoxy of *Pearl*, 603–4," *Modern Language Notes*, LVIII [1943], 370–72); D. W. Robertson ("The 'Heresy' of the *Pearl*," *Modern Language Notes*, LXV [1950], 152–55); Sister Mary Vincent Hillmann ("*Pearl*, 382: 'Mare reȝ mysse'?" *Modern Language Notes*, LXVIII [1953], 528–31, and "*Pearl*: Inlyche and Rewarde,"

Modern Language Notes, LVI [1941], 457–58); Elizabeth Hart ("The Heaven of Virgins," *Modern Language Notes*, XLII [1927], 113–16); James R. Sledd ("Three Textual Notes on Fourteenth-Century Poetry," *Modern Language Notes*, LV [1940], 379–82); and G. G. Coulton (*Medieval Panorama* [Cambridge, Eng., 1938], p. 220.)

36. Dorothy L. Sayers, *Introductory Papers on Dante* (New York, 1954), p. 57.

37. "A Hymn of St. Ephrem." See *The Pearl*, ed. Sister Mary Vincent Hillmann (New York, 1961), p. 108.

38. See Howard R. Patch, *The Other World, According to Descriptions in Medieval Literature* (Cambridge, Mass., 1950).

39. Johnson, p. 169.

40. *Ibid.*

41. Joseph Campbell, *The Hero with a Thousand Faces* (New York, 1949), pp. 49–59.

42. *Ibid.*, p. 10.

43. Arnold Toynbee, *A Study of History*, abridged by D. C. Somervell (Oxford, 1947), p. 217.

44. Johnson, p. 161.

45. *Pearl*, ed. Gordon, p. xviii.

46. *Ibid.*, p. 72.

47. For the relationship of the poem to the *consolatio* tradition see John Conley ("*Pearl* and a Lost Tradition," *Journal of English and Germanic Philology*, LIV [1955], 332–47) and V. E. Watts ("*Pearl* as a Consolatio," *Medium Aevum*, XXXII [1963], 34–36).

48. I cannot, however, pursue this argument to its furthest conclusion, as do John Conley and Sister Mary Vincent Hillmann (*The Pearl*), and identify the pearl with a material and thus transient earthly good, the loss of which has plunged the narrator, who is *homo animalis* blinded by avarice, into an unreasonable grief from which he is rescued by the counsels of the maiden who returns to him his "true pearl," his own soul, which he had lost.

CHAPTER THREE

1. Ed. by Sir I. Gollancz (London, 1913) and Hartley Bateson (2nd ed., rev., Manchester, 1918). The poem is also included in *Early English Alliterative Poems*, ed. by R. Morris for the Early English Text Society (Original Series, No. 1) in 1864. The line references in the text and notes of this chapter are to Bateson's edition.

2. Most of the translation in this chapter is that of Jessie L. Weston in *Romance, Vision and Satire* (Boston, 1912). A few passages are my own translations.

3. According to Bernhard ten Brink (*A History of English Literature*, trans. H. M. Kennedy [New York, 1889]), Sir Israel Gollancz

(*The Cambridge History of English Literature* [London, 1910], I), and a few other early critics, *Patience* records the poet's final reconciliation to the death of his daughter recounted in *Pearl*, which by this theory is the second of his poems.

4. For a summary of the evidence, cf. Robert Menner, ed., *Purity, A Middle English Poem* (New Haven, 1920), pp. xxx–xxxviii.

5. Bateson, p. xiii, n. 3.

6. See particularly Menner, p. xxix, and Bateson, p. xxvii.

7. Jonah 1:17.

8. Jonah 3:10.

9. For a full discussion, see Bateson, pp. xli–xlvi.

10. Edwin Dodge Cuffe, S.J., "An Interpretation of *Patience, Cleanness,* and *The Pearl* from the Viewpoint of Imagery" (unpublished dissertation, University of North Carolina, 1951), p. 67.

11. *Ibid.*, p. 61.

12. *Ibid.*, p. 67.

13. Cf. the references given by Jacques-Paul Migne, *Patrologia Latinae,* under the heading "Jonas."

14. Matt. 12:38–41.

15. Fr. Cuffe (pp. 78–9) attempts to find a connection between the patristical use of Jonah as a type of Christ and the poet's use of the whale's mouth as an image of the "hell-mouth" of the mystery plays, but the point is strained.

16. *Ibid.*, p. 67.

17. Joseph B. Zavadil, "A Study of Meaning in *Patience* and *Cleanness*" (unpublished dissertation, Stanford University, 1961).

18. While I would of course like to be able to establish beyond any sort of doubt that the poem deliberately echoes the composition and structure of the medieval sermon, the great variations in pulpit oratory in the period make such a case nearly impossible to prove to everyone's satisfaction, though I myself am convinced that the poet is consciously making use of sermon form.

In general, the medieval sermon involves six possible divisions: *theme, protheme, dilation, exemplum, peroration,* and *closing formula.* But no sermon apparently was expected to use all of these, and C. S. Baldwin's chapter on preaching in *Medieval Rhetoric and Poetic* (New York, 1928) makes it clear that the composition of a medieval sermon was subject only to the most general and flexible of principles. Certainly *Patience* can be said, and this optimistically, to utilize only (1) *theme* (l. 1), and this in only a very general sense, since normally the term "theme" refers to the announcing and translating of a scriptural text; (2) *protheme* (ll. 2–8), the preacher's general introduction to his task; (3) *dilation* (ll. 9–60), an expansion of the theme, in this case by means of definition and citation (see Baldwin, p. 237); (4)

exemplum (ll. 61–523), the Jonah story; and (5) *peroration* (ll. 524–30), the closing application of the theme. The poem ends not with the conventional closing tag (*qui vivit et regnat,* etc.), but with a return to theme.

19. J. M. Manly's notes to "The Pardoner's Tale" in his one-volume edition of *The Canterbury Tales* (New York, 1928), p. 614.

CHAPTER FOUR

1. Richard Morris in *Early English Alliterative Poems,* Early English Text Society, Original Series 1 (London, 1864), p. xiii. However, I am in agreement with C. G. Osgood (ed.), *The Pearl* (Boston, 1906), p. viii, and Robert Menner (ed.), *Purity* (New Haven, 1920) that *Purity* is a "more accurate and appropriate" title for the poem. The line numbers in my text are to Menner's edition. The translations are my own.

2. See the evidence presented by Menner, pp. xxx–xxxviii.

3. Edwin Dodge Cuffe, S.J., "An Interpretation of *Patience, Cleanness* and *The Pearl,* from the Viewpoint of Imagery" (unpublished dissertation, University of North Carolina, 1951), p. 113.

4. The use in *Patience* of Tertullian's *De Jona* is highly doubtful.

5. Menner, p. xxxix.

6. *Ibid.,* p. xlii.

7. *Ibid.,* p. xl.

8. *Ibid.*

9. For a full discussion of the imagery of the poem, see Fr. Cuffe's dissertation.

10. Cuffe, p. 138.

CHAPTER FIVE

1. For a listing of the principal editions of the poem, see the general bibliography, pp. 131 and 132.

2. Throughout this chapter, I have quoted Theodore Howard Banks, Jr.'s translation (New York, 1929).

3. See p. 108 below.

4. Dorothy Everett, quoted in *A Handbook to Literature,* ed. Thrall, Hibbard, and Holman (New York, 1960), p. 278.

5. See Charles Moorman, *A Knyght There Was* (Lexington, Ky., 1967), pp. 27–57.

6. For the Bannatyne Club in 1839.

7. Laurita L. Hill, "Madden's Divisions of *Sir Gawain* and the 'Large Initial Capitals' of Cotton Nero A.x.," *Speculum,* XXI (1946), 67–71.

8. The presence of which, by the way, was remarked upon by Mad-

den and by Tolkien and Gordon in their editions of the poem, but not followed up in either case.

9. Dale B. J. Randall, "A Note on Structure in *Sir Gawain and the Green Knight*," *Modern Language Notes*, LXXII (1957), 161–63.

10. M. R. Watson, "The Chronology of *Sir Gawain and the Green Knight*," *Modern Language Notes*, LXIV (1949), 84–86.

11. *The Gawain-Poet: Studies in His Personality and Background* (Chapel Hill, 1956), pp. 31–48.

12. *A Study of Gawain and the Green Knight* (Cambridge, Mass., 1916).

13. For a thorough history of the development of the legend as it appears in the early chronicles, see R. H. Fletcher, *The Arthurian Materials in the Chronicles* (Boston, 1906).

14. See R. S. Loomis, *Celtic Myth and Arthurian Romance* (New York, 1927), for a clear statement of the Celticist point of view. Prof. Loomis's many later articles should also be consulted for specific derivations of Arthurian characters and situations from Celtic sources.

15. Since there are a great many more early written legends in Irish than in Welsh folklore and since both presumably stem from the same antecedents, Celtic scholars frequently resort to Irish written records to supplement their knowledge of Welsh myth.

16. Larry D. Benson, "The Source of the Beheading Episode in *Sir Gawain and the Green Knight*," *Modern Philology*, LIX (1961), 1–12.

17. Laura Hibbard Loomis, "Gawain and the Green Knight," *Arthurian Literature in the Middle Ages* (London, 1959), pp. 535–36.

18. J. R. R. Tolkien and E. V. Gordon (eds.), *Sir Gawain and the Green Knight* (Oxford, 1946), xiv.

19. J. R. Hulbert, "Syr Gawayn and the Grene Knyȝt," *Modern Philology*, XIII (1915–16), 433–62, 689–730.

20. Else von Schaubert, *Der Englische Ursprung von "Syr Gawayn and the Grene Knyȝt*," *Englische Studien*, LVII (1923), 330–446.

21. Sir Israel Gollancz, Mabel Day, and Mary S. Serjeantson (eds.), *Sir Gawain and the Green Knight*, Early English Text Society, 210 (London, 1940), p. xxxii.

22. Alice Buchanan, "The Irish Framework of *Gawain and the Green Knight*," *PMLA*, XLVII (1932), 315–338.

23. L. H. Loomis, p. 536.

24. *Ibid.*, p. 531.

25. R. S. Loomis, "More Celtic Elements in *Gawain and the Green Knight*," *Journal of English and Germanic Philology*, XLII (1943), 149–184.

26. Esp. W. A. Nitze ("Is the Green Knight a Vegetation Myth?" *Modern Philology*, XXXIII [1936], 351–66) and E. K. Chambers (*The Medieval Stage* [London, 1903], I, 185–186).

27. John Speirs, *Medieval English Poetry: The Non-Chaucerian Tradition* (London, 1957), p. 219.

28. Francis Berry, "*Sir Gawayne and the Grene Knight*" in *The Age of Chaucer, A Guide to English Literature I* (London, 1954), p. 158.

29. R. S. Loomis, *Arthurian Tradition and Chrétien de Troyes* (New York, 1949), p. 279.

30. Ananda Coomaraswamy, "*Sir Gawain and the Green Knight:* Indra and Namuci," *Speculum,* XIX (1944), 104–125.

31. Heinrich Zimmer, *The King and the Corpse* (Washington, 1948).

32. A. H. Krappe, "Who *Was* the Green Knight?" *Speculum,* XIII (1938), 206–15.

33. Dale B. J. Randall, "Was the Green Knight a Fiend?" *Studies in Philology,* LVII (1960), 479–91.

34. Haldeen Braddy, "Sir Gawain and Ralph Holmes the Green Knight," *Modern Language Notes,* LXVII (1952), 240–42.

35. J. R. L. Highfield, "The Green Squire," *Medium Aevum,* XXII (1953), 18–23.

36. Isaac Jackson, "*Sir Gawain* Considered as a 'Garter' Poem," *Anglia,* XXXVII (1913), 393–423.

37. Hulbert, pp. 699 ff.

38. Kittredge, pp. 129–30.

39. Marie Borroff, *Sir Gawain and the Green Knight: A Stylistic and Metrical Study* (New Haven, 1962), p. 128. For discussions of the *Pearl*-poet's use of the rhetorical and metrical traditions of the Middle Ages, see also Derek A. Pearsall, "Rhetorical 'Descriptio' in *Sir Gawain and the Green Knight,*" *Modern Language Review,* L (1955), 129–34.

40. See p. 101 above.

41. The vegetation myth is by and large the most popular of the theories of myth applied to *Sir Gawain and the Green Knight* and the most relevant. Theories, such as those of Krappe, Zimmer, and Coomaraswamy, which see in the poem the hero's conquest of death (roughly identified with the Green Knight) would seem to rank next in popularity.

42. Speirs, p. 220.

43. *Ibid.,* p. 218.

44. Morton W. Bloomfield, "*Sir Gawain and the Green Knight:* An Appraisal," *PMLA,* LXXVI (1961), 13. Bloomfield's article contains a very full summary of recent criticism and scholarship.

45. The most comprehensive of the new approaches to the poem, that of Hans Schnyder (*Sir Gawain and the Green Knight* [Basel, 1961]), rejects Speirs's theory on the ground that it brings to bear the patterns of pre-Christian myth upon an obviously Christian poem. Yet

Schnyder's attempt—based for the most part upon the charity-cupidity dichotomy of the new school of scriptural exegesis—to make the poem conform to the four-fold allegorical pattern of *The Divine Comedy,* although containing some excellent insights into the kingship of Arthur and the role of Fortune in the poem, never quite comes off. The ordinary reader, even in the poet's time, would never, I think, have identified the Green Knight allegorically as the word of God and anagogically as Christ, an identification central to Snyder's interpretation.

46. Kittredge, p. 132.

47. Hulbert, p. 454.

48. Denver E. Baughan, "The Role of Morgan le Fay in *Sir Gawain and the Green Knight,*" *ELH,* XVII (1950), 241–51.

49. Albert B. Friedham, "Morgan le Fay in *Sir Gawain and the Green Knight,*" *Speculum,* XXXV (1960), 274.

50. Mother Angela Carson, "Morgain la Fee as the Principle of Unity in *Gawain and the Green Knight,*" *Modern Language Quarterly,* XXIII (1962), 3–16.

51. Alan M. Markman, "The Meaning of *Sir Gawain and the Green Knight,*" *PMLA,* LXXII (1957), 575.

52. Richard Hamilton Green, "Gawain's Shield and the Quest for Perfection," *ELH,* XXIX (1962), 138.

53. George J. Englehardt, "The Predicament of Gawain," *Modern Language Quarterly,* XVI (1955), 224–25.

54. John Burrow, "The Two Confession Scenes in *Sir Gawain and the Green Knight,*" *Modern Philology,* LVII (1959), 73–79.

55. Robert W. Ackerman, "Gawain's Shield: Penitential Doctrine in *Gawain and the Green Knight,*" *Anglia,* LXXVI (1958), 254–65.

56. G. V. Smithers, "What *Sir Gawain and the Green Knyght* is About," *Medium Aevum,* XXXII (1963), 171–89.

57. Baughan, *op. cit.* It is possible to object to this general line of argument by pointing out that this sort of religious imagery is usual in the medieval romance. However, *Sir Gawain and the Green Knight* is in structure, tone, and imagery far more tightly constructed than the usual romance, so tightly constructed in fact that it would be dangerous to pass off any one of the poem's myriad details as "merely" traditional. What is most apparent in *Sir Gawain and the Green Knight,* even upon the most cursory reading, is that here, as in Chaucer, merely traditional elements become meaningful and functional when set by the author in the new context of the poem. The *Gawain* poet thus adapts the conventional and largely meaningless religious imagery surrounding the chivalric quest to his own purposes in defining the truly religious nature of Gawain's journey. It seems clear to me also that despite Speirs, Loomis, Weston, *et al.* to the contrary, the *Gawain* poet is a Christian writer, not a Druid in disguise. There

is nothing in the poem, aside from the hero pattern which is universal and thus Christian as well as Celtic, which the poet could not have taken directly from the Christian tradition.

58. The general strain of religious imagery which runs through the poem serves to reinforce this interpretation of the spiritual nature of Gawain's quest. Mass is heard daily in the castles of both Arthur and Bercilak. Gawain calls three times upon God to aid him in undertaking the quest (390, 399, 549). Arthur's court commends Gawain to God's protection on his departure (596), and Gawain, having thanked "Jesus and Julian" for his safe arrival at Bercilak's castle (774), blesses the porter who welcomes him there (869). Bercilak's court rejoices that God has sent Gawain to them to be a model of courtly behavior (920 ff.). Gawain commends Bercilak to God's grace (1038 ff.). The interviews with Bercilak's lady are filled with oaths and commendations to Christ. Upon leaving, Gawain commends Bercilak's castle to Christ (2067) and blesses and is blessed by the porter of Bercilak's castle (2071 ff.). Bercilak and Gawain, after the conclusion of the beheading game, "each other commend / To the Prince of Paradise" (2472–73).

59. William Goldhurst, "The Green and the Gold: The Major Theme of *Gawain and the Green Knight*," *College English*, XX (1958), 61. See also John S. Lewis, "*Gawain and the Green Knight*," *College English*, XXI (1959), 50–51.

60. Bloomfield, p. 16.

61. "Pure and Impure Poetry," *The Kenyon Review*, V (1943), 232.

CHAPTER SIX

1. Marie Borroff's book, *Sir Gawain and the Green Knight: A Stylistic and Metrical Study* (New Haven, 1962), despite its hesitancy to generalize, is a fine beginning in this direction.

Selected Bibliography

PRIMARY SOURCES
(Principal Editions of the Works
of the *Pearl*-poet)

1. *Collected Editions*

GOLLANCZ, SIR ISRAEL. *Pearl, Cleanness, Patience, and Sir Gawain, Reproduced in Facsimile from the Unique Ms. Cotton Nero A.x. in the British Museum.* Early English Text Society, Original Series 162. London: Oxford University Press, 1923. An excellently reproduced facsimile of the manuscript.

MORRIS, RICHARD (ed.). *Early English Alliterative Poems in the West Midland Dialect of the Fourteenth Century.* Early English Text Society, Original Series I. London: Oxford University Press, 1864. This first "modern" edition contains *Pearl, Purity* (called here *Cleanness*), and *Patience.*

2. Pearl

GOLLANCZ, SIR ISRAEL (ed.). *Pearl.* Edited with Modern Rendering. London: Chatto and Windus, 1921. A provocative edition, marked by the editor's numerous deviations from the manuscript.

GORDON, ERIC V. (ed.). *Pearl* (rev. IDA L. GORDON). London: Oxford University Press, 1953. The fullest and most conservative edition, with critical apparatus and selected bibliography which includes a section on structure and theme.

HILLMANN, SISTER MARY VINCENT (ed.). *The Pearl. Text with a Literal Translation and Interpretation.* New York: University Publishers, 1961. Contains a particularly good set of notes, especially on the theological issues raised by the poem.

OSGOOD, CHARLES G. (ed.). *The Pearl. A Middle English Poem.* Boston: D. C. Heath & Co., 1906. Notable for its full and sensible introduction.

3. Patience

BATESON, HARTLEY. *Patience.* Manchester: University of Manchester Press, 1912. Second edition, 1918. Bateson's first edition contains a number of inaccuracies. The second edition, though no longer in print, is the most accessible text of the poem.

GOLLANCZ, SIR ISRAEL (ed.). *Patience, An Alliterative Version of Jonah by the Poet of Pearl.* Select Early English Poems, I. London: Oxford University Press, 1913. Second edition, 1924. Like all of Gollancz's editions, an extremely liberal reading of the text.

4. Purity

GOLLANCZ, SIR ISRAEL (ed.). *Cleanness, An Alliterative Tripartite Poem on the Deluge, the Destruction of Sodom, and the Death of Belshazzar, by the Poet of Pearl.* London: Oxford University Press, 1921. Contains the text of the poem, arranged in quatrains, and Gollancz's notes.

————. *Cleanness, Glossary and Illustrative Texts.* Select Early English Poems, IX. London: Oxford University Press, 1933. Actually constitutes the second volume of Gollancz's 1921 edition and contains passages from the poet's sources.

MENNER, ROBERT J. (ed.). *Purity, A Middle English Poem.* Yale Studies in English, LXI. New Haven: Yale University Press, 1920. Though out of print, the best edition available. Full introduction and notes.

5. Sir Gawain and the Green Knight

GOLLANCZ, SIR ISRAEL (ed.). *Sir Gawain and the Green Knight.* Introductory Essays by MABEL DAY and MARY S. SERJEANTSON. Early English Text Society, Original Series 210. London: Oxford University Press, 1940. The best available edition, though the reader must watch for Gollancz's texual eccentricities.

TOLKIEN, J. R. R. and E. V. GORDON, (eds.). *Sir Gawain and the Green Knight.* Oxford: The Clarendon Press, 1946. A more conservative text than Gollancz's. Good general introduction and notes.

SECONDARY SOURCES

This bibliography is designed to direct the attention of the general reader to the major works concerning the *Pearl*-poet. Therefore, it lists only a fraction of the nearly three hundred items devoted to the author and his poems.

Two major principles of selection have been followed: (1) general and interpretative studies, rather than articles (valuable as they are) dealing only with technical minutiae of particular words and phrases, have been given priority and (2) recent studies, most of which make some attempt as a matter of course at summarizing older studies in the same area, have often been included instead of older and less relevant studies.

Restrictions in space make impossible any system of duplication or cross-reference of items. A work listed in the *Pearl* section may thus very well contain a few valuable remarks on *Sir Gawain and the Green Knight.* This is particularly true of the introductions to the editions of the several poems. While I have tried to point out such cases in the annotations, they will nevertheless go unnoticed by the reader who searches only under a single heading.

1. *The Author*

BRADDY, HALDEEN. "Sir Gawain and Ralph Holmes the Green Knight," *Modern Language Notes,* LXVII (1952), 240–42. Suggests that the nickname of a captain of the White Companies who was decapitated in Spain may have influenced the *Pearl*-poet.

BROWN, CARLETON F. "Note on the Question of Strode's Authorship of *The Pearl,*" *PMLA,* XIX (1904), 146–48. Demonstrates that Gollancz confused the Ralph Strode of Merton College, a noted logician, with a Ralph Strode traditionally spoken of as a poet and with a lawyer of that name who lived in Aldersgate, London, to produce a wholly fictional Ralph Strode of his own devising.

CARGILL, OSCAR, and MARGARET SCHLAUCH. "*The Pearl* and its Jeweller," *PMLA,* XLIII (1928), 105–23. Proposes that the poem was written on the death of Margaret (daughter of John Hastings, Earl of Pembroke, and Margaret, daughter of Edward III) and that the author was one of five secular clerks attached to the Pembroke household.

CHAPMAN, C. O. "The Authorship of the *Pearl,*" *PMLA,* XLVII (1932), 346–53. Proposes as author of *Pearl* John of Erghome, an Augustinian Friar of York, author of the Latin *Prophesy of John Bridlington.*

———. "Chaucer and the Gawain-Poet: A Conjecture," *Modern Language Notes,* LXVIII (1953), 521–24. Compares the narrative in the first part of the Squire's Tale with *Gawain,* revealing at least nine points of agreement in the order of events and the conduct of the characters.

———. "The Musical Training of the *Pearl* Poet," *PMLA,* XLVI (1931), 177–81. Illustrates from all four poems the wide knowledge of music of different kinds possessed by the poet.

———. "Virgil and the Gawain Poet," *PMLA,* LX (1945), 16–23. Maintains that the *Pearl*-poet had read the *Aeneid* and imitated certain features of it. Also lists as other works read by the poet the Vulgate, *Romance of the Rose,* the French text of Mande-

ville, the *Divine Comedy,* Boccaccio's *Olympia,* and Boethius'
Consolation of Philosophy.

EVERETT, DOROTHY and NAOMI D. HURNARD. "Legal Phraseology in
a Passage in *Pearl,*" *Medium Aevum,* XVI (1947), 9–15. Shows
author's familiarity with legal terms of the period.

G. P. J. "The Author of *Sir Gawain and the Green Knight,*" *Notes and
Queries,* New Series III (1956), 53–54. From the description of
Gawain's journey from Wales to the Wirral concludes that the
poet must have been familiar with the country.

GOLLANCZ, SIR ISRAEL. *"Pearl, Cleanness, Patience,* and *Sir Gawayne,*"
Cambridge History of English Literature. New York: G. P. Put-
nam's Sons, 1907. Vol. I. Puts forward an interesting, though untenable, hypothetical biography based on the poems.

NEILSON, GEORGE. *Huchown of the Awle Ryale, the Alliterative Poet:
A Historical Criticism of Fourteenth Century Poems Ascribed to
Sir Hew of Eglintoun.* Glasgow: J. MacLehose and Sons, 1902.
Unconvincingly ascribes the works of the *Pearl*-poet to Huchown.

SAVAGE, HENRY LYTTLETON. *The* Gawain-*Poet: Studies in His Personality and Background.* Chapel Hill, N. C.: University of North
Carolina Press, 1956. Treats the poet as to profession, place of
origin, and status. Identifies the poet as a clerk in the household
of Enguerrand de Coucy.

WINTERMUTE, E. "The *Pearl's* Author as Herbalist," *Modern Language
Notes,* LXIV (1949), 83–84. Uses the *Pearl*-poet's use of the
herb "gromwell" to identify his profession as that of an apothecary.

2. *The Author's Times*

BAUGH, ALBERT C. "The Alliterative Revival," *A Literary History of
England.* New York: Appleton-Century-Crofts, Inc., 1948. Discusses the Alliterative Revival generally—the area involved, date,
and characteristics of the poems produced during the course of it.

EVERETT, DOROTHY. *Essays on Middle English Literature.* London:
Oxford University Press, 1955. Contains nine essays, including
three papers on the Alliterative Revival which, together with one
chapter on Layamon, were projected chapters of the Middle English volume of the *Oxford History of English Literature.* Treats
works of the *Pearl*-poet with sanity and sensitivity.

HULBERT, J. R. "A Hypothesis Concerning the Alliterative Revival,"
Modern Philology, XXVIII (1931), 405–22. Suggests that an
audience for Alliterative Revival poetry may have existed among
the adherents of the "baronial opposition" to the Crown.

OAKDEN, J. P. *Alliterative Poetry in Middle English.* 2 vols. Manchester: Manchester University Press, 1930–35. A comprehensive
survey, though somewhat dated.

WELLS, J. E. *Manual of the Writings in Middle English.* New Haven: Yale University Press, 1916. With nine supplements to 1951. Invaluable for summaries and bibliographies.

3. *The Author's Language*

HULBERT, J. R. "The 'West Midland' of the Romances," *Modern Philology,* XIX (1921), 1–16. Disputes the traditional assignment of *Sir Gawain and the Green Knight,* and of the alliterative romances generally, to the West Midland dialect of Middle English.

MENNER, ROBERT J. "Four Notes on the West Midland Dialect," *Modern Language Notes,* XLI (1926), 454–58. Points out that certain word forms and letters are found particularly in the West and Northwest Midland dialects.

――――. "*Sir Gawain and the Green Knight* and the West Midland," *PMLA,* XXXVII (1922), 503–26. Refutes Hulbert's (*Modern Philology,* XIX) argument as far as it concerns *Gawain,* showing that there is sufficient evidence to assign the poem to the Northwest rather than to the Northeast Midland dialect.

SERJEANTSON, M. S. "The Dialects of the West Midlands in Middle English," *Review of English Studies,* III (1927), 54–67, 186–203, 319–31. Attempts to separate and define these early dialects. Contains references to the *Pearl*-poet.

4. *The Unity of the Four Poems*

CLARK, JOHN W. "Observations on Certain Differences in Vocabulary between *Cleanness* and *Sir Gawain and the Green Knight,*" *Philological Quarterly,* XXVIII (1949), 261–73. Questions, as do the following three articles, the mutual authorship of the poems of Cotton Nero A.x. on the basis of differences in words and usages.

――――. "On Certain 'Alliterative' and 'Poetic' Words in the Poems Attributed to 'The *Gawain*-Poet,'" *Modern Language Quarterly,* XII (1951), 387–98.

――――. "Paraphrases for 'God' in the Poems Attributed to 'The *Gawain*-Poet,'" *Modern Language Notes,* LXV (1950), 232–36.

――――. "The *Gawain*-Poet and the Substantival Adjective," *Journal of English and Germanic Philology,* XLIX (1950), 60–66.

EBBS, JOHN DALE, "Stylistic Mannerisms of the *Gawain*-Poet," *Journal of English and Germanic Philology,* LVII (1958), 522–25. Supports the theory of common authorship for *Patience, Purity, Pearl,* and *Sir Gawain* by pointing out stylistic mannerisms included in all four poems.

5. Pearl

BLOOMFIELD, MORTON W. "Symbolism in Medieval Literature," *Modern Philology*, LVI (1958), 73–81. Attacks the multi-level approach.

BROWN, CARLETON F. "The Author of *Pearl*, Considered in the Light of His Theological Opinions," *PMLA*, XIX (1904), 115–45. Presents the poet as a learned ecclesiastic opposing the grades of reward defined by Jerome, Augustine, and Gregory.

CHAMBERS, EDMUND K. *English Literature at the Close of the Middle Ages*. London: Oxford University Press, 1945. Suggests *Pearl* as an example of concatenation and shows linking of stanzas by repetition or variation.

CONLEY, JOHN. "*Pearl* and a Lost Tradition," *Journal of English and Germanic Philology*, LIV (1955), 332–47. Offers an interpretation of *Pearl* as a Christian *consolatio*, analogous in theme, situation, and treatment to Boethius's *Consolation of Philosophy*.

COULTON, G. G. *Medieval Panorama*. Cambridge: Cambridge University Press, 1938. Indicates Dante followed scholastic teaching of gradation of perfection in bliss of souls in Heaven.

CUFFE, EDWIN DODGE, S.J. "An Interpretation of *Patience, Cleanness*, and *The Pearl* from the Viewpoint of Imagery." Unpublished Ph.D. dissertation, University of North Carolina, 1951. Gives a detailed study of the large focal images in all three poems.

FLETCHER, J. B. "The Allegory of the *Pearl*," *Journal of English and Germanic Philology*, XX (1921), 1–21. Views the work as both elegy and allegory.

GARRETT, ROBERT MAX. "The *Pearl*: An Interpretation," University of Washington *Studies in English*, IV (1918), 1–48. Uses Eucharistic teachings to explain the symbolism in *Pearl*.

GREENE, W. K. "The *Pearl*: A New Interpretation," *PMLA*, XL (1925), 814–27. Contends the lost child in infancy is a fictional, literary device used to present a lesson in "divine grace."

HAMILTON, MARIE PADGETT. "The Meaning of the Middle English *Pearl*," *PMLA*, LXX (1955), 805–24. Considers the pearl a regenerate soul, made so by baptism and God's favor.

HART, ELIZABETH. "The Heaven of Virgins," *Modern Language Notes*, XLII (1927), 113–16. Contends with Sister Madeleva concerning a two-year-old's appearance among the 144,000 virgins.

HILLMANN, SISTER MARY VINCENT. "Some Debatable Words in *Pearl* and its Theme," *Modern Language Notes*, LX (1945), 241–48. States theme of jeweler first prizing a pearl above spiritual welfare, then losing it, and finally becoming conscious of the truly great value—the beauty of the immortal soul.

HOFFMAN, STANTON DE VOREN. "The *Pearl:* Notes for an Interpretation," *Modern Philology,* LVIII (1960), 73–80. Believes the poem basically an elegy and proclaims its theme a spiritual adventure of the soul.

JOHNSON, WENDELL STACY. "The Imagery and Diction of the *Pearl:* Toward an Interpretation," *ELH,* XX (1953), 161–80. Emphasizes imagery (world of growing things, light, and blood and water) and plot (three divisions using dream allegory device).

LUTTRELL, C. A. "The Medieval Tradition of the Pearl Virginity," *Medium Aevum,* XXXI (1962), 194–200. Traces pearl as symbol of virginity.

MCANDREW, BRUNO. "*The Pearl,* A Catholic *Paradise Lost,*" *American Benedictine Review,* VIII (1957), 243–51. Discounts literalistic view and emphasizes the mystical "reflections of the interior life"; personifies pearl as Paradise, which Everyman has lost through sin.

MADELEVA, SISTER MARY. *Pearl: A Study in Spiritual Dryness.* New York: D. Appleton and Co., 1925. Interprets the poem as an exposition of spiritual dryness or interior desolation.

MEDARY, MARGARET P. "Stanza-linking in Middle English Verse," *Romanic Review,* VII (1916), 243–70. Includes discussion of *Pearl* in a general discussion of stanza-linking techniques.

MOORMAN, CHARLES. "The Role of the Narrator in *Pearl,*" *Modern Philology,* LIII (1955), 73–81. Considers the work elegiac in theme and structure.

PATCH, HOWARD R. *The Other World, According to Descriptions in Medieval Literature.* Cambridge, Mass.: Harvard University Press, 1950. Shows "otherworld reminiscence" in the dream mechanism used in *Pearl.*

ROBERTSON, D. W. "The 'Heresy' of *The Pearl,*" *Modern Language Notes,* LXV (1950), 152–55. Shows poet does not run counter to St. Augustine's teaching; believes *Pearl*-poet indicates that anyone, through repentance, may attain spiritual purity and receive the consequent reward.

———. "The Pearl as a Symbol," *Modern Language Notes,* LXV (1950), 155–61. Sees the poem from the viewpoint of medieval exegesis on four levels.

SCHOLFIELD, W. H. "The Nature and Fabric of *The Pearl,*" *PMLA,* XIX (1904), 154–215. Presents the first view of *Pearl* as a didactic allegory; believes pearl to be a figment of the author's imagination.

———. "Symbolism, Allegory, and Autobiography in *The Pearl,*" *PMLA,* XXIV (1909), 585–675. Believes symbolism pervasive, not intermittent, that the theme of the poem is purity, and that the allegory proper deals with the Pearl of Great Price.

SPEARING, A. C. "Symbolic and Dramatic Development in *Pearl*," *Modern Philology*, LX, 1 (1962), 1–12. Considers a non-allegorical approach; thinks dreamer unable to follow symbolism of pearl-maiden.

STERN, MILTON R. "An Approach to *The Pearl*," *Journal of English and Germanic Philology*, LIV (1955), 684–92. Makes use of the conventions of scriptural exegesis and the lapidary tradition in order to frame a four-fold interpretation.

WATTS, V. E. "*Pearl* as a Consolatio," *Medium Aevum*, XXXII (1963), 34–36. Cites examples of the *consolatio* used as an instructional device by St. Ambrose, St. Jerome, and St. Paulinus of Nola.

WELLEK, RENÉ. "*The Pearl*: An Interpretation of the Middle-English Poem," Charles University *Studies in English*, IV (1933), 1–33. Considers reason for and lesson of *Pearl* more important than genre.

6. Sir Gawain and the Green Knight

ACKERMAN, ROBERT W. "Gawain's Shield: Penitential Doctrine in *Gawain and the Green Knight*," *Anglia*, LXXVI (1958), 254–65. Finds echoes of the confessional in the description of the pentangle.

BAUGHAM, DENVER E. "The Role of Morgan le Fay in *Sir Gawain and the Green Knight*," *ELH*, XVII (1950), 241–51. Attempts to show, first, that Morgan le Fay's plan succeeds, and secondly, that through Gawain's chastity the beheading episode constitutes an organic part of both the theme and the action.

BENSON, LARRY D. "The Source of the Beheading Episode in *Sir Gawain and the Green Knight*," *Modern Philology*, LIX (1961), 1–12. Argues that the direct source of the beheading episode in *Sir Gawain and the Green Knight* is *Le Livre de Caradoc*.

BERRY, FRANCIS. "*Sir Gawayne and the Grene Knight*," *The Age of Chaucer, A Guide to English Literature I*, ed. BORIS FORD. Harmondsworth: Penguin Books, 1954. Follows Speirs in stressing mythic elements.

BLOOMFIELD, MORTON W. "*Sir Gawain and the Green Knight*: An Appraisal," *PMLA*, LXXVI (1961), 7–19. Comprehensively reviews the scholarship and problems connected with the poem.

BORROFF, MARIE. *Sir Gawain and the Green Knight: A Stylistic and Metrical Study*. New Haven: Yale University Press, 1962. Examines the poet's use of the rhetorical conventions of the period.

BOWERS, R. H. " '*Gawain and the Green Knyght*' as Entertainment," *Modern Language Quarterly*, XXIV (1963), 333–41. Rejects current mythical and ethical theories.

BUCHANAN, ALICE. "The Irish Framework of *Gawain and the Green Knight,*" *PMLA*, XLVII (1932), 315–38. Finds in the *Carl of Carlisle* and two other Arthurian episodes examples of the challenge and temptation motives which Kittredge believed were found combined only in *Sir Gawain and the Green Knight.*

BURROW, JOHN. "The Two Confession Scenes in *Sir Gawain and the Green Knight,*" *Modern Philology*, LVII (1959), 73–79. Traces penitential doctrine in the poem by examining the so-called "confession" scenes.

CARSON, MOTHER ANGELA. "Morgain la Fee as the Principle of Unity in *Gawain and the Green Knight,*" *Modern Language Quarterly*, XXIII (1962), 3–16. Attempts to show that by a study of the text and an awareness of tradition, Morgain will be seen to emerge as the most significant character in the poem.

COOMARASWAMY, ANANDA K. "*Sir Gawain and the Green Knight:* Indra and Namuci," *Speculum*, XIX (1944), 104–25. Finds parallels in Indian myth and ritual to certain features of the beheading incident.

ENGELHARDT, GEORGE J. "The Predicament of Gawain," *Modern Language Quarterly*, XVI (1955), 218–25. Discusses the symbolic and ethical importance of the pentangle and the knot of green silk.

FRIEDMAN, ALBERT B. "Morgan le Fay in *Sir Gawain and the Green Knight,*" *Speculum*, XXXV (1960), 260–74. Rejects Baughan's theory of the role of Morgan le Fay.

GOLDHURST, WILLIAM. "The Green and the Gold: The Major Theme of *Gawain and the Green Knight,*" *College English*, XX (1958), 61–65. Argues that "the major theme of *Sir Gawain and the Green Knight* is the idea that the primitive and sometimes brutal forces of nature make known their demands to all men, even to those who would take shelter behind the civilized comforts of court life."

GREEN, R. H. "Gawain's Shield and the Quest for Perfection," *ELH*, XXIX (1962), 121–39. Examines some of the implications of the poem's comic tone for its central concern with the ideal of secular perfection.

HILL, LAURITA L. "Madden's Divisions of *Sir Gawain* and the 'Large Initial Capitals' of *Cotton Nero A.x.*" *Speculum*, XXI (1946), 67–71. Finds Madden's divisons not supported by manuscript evidence.

HULBERT, J. R. "Syr Gawayn and the Grene Knyȝt," *Modern Philology*, XIII (1915–16), 433–62, 689–730. Discovers the sources of the poem in ancient Celtic fairy lore.

JACKSON, ISAAC. "*Sir Gawain* Considered as a 'Garter' Poem," *Anglia,* XXXVII (1913), 393–423. Connects *Gawain* with the foundation of the Order of the Garter.

KITTREDGE, G. L. *A Study of Gawain and the Green Knight.* Cambridge: Harvard University Press, 1916. Proposes that the poem contains two motifs—the Beheading Game and the Temptation —inherited from Celtic myth and first combined in a lost French romance, the immediate source of *Sir Gawain and the Green Knight.*

KRAPPE, A. H. "Who *Was* the Green Knight?" *Speculum,* XIII (1938), 206–15. Identifies the Green Knight with the Lord of Hades.

LEWIS, JOHN S. "*Gawain and the Green Knight,*" *College English,* XXI (1959), 50–51. Maintains that green and gold traditionally symbolize vanishing youth. "The juxtaposition of the youthful king and company and the Green Knight is . . . another example of the poet's skill in counter-balancing opposite moods."

LOOMIS, R. S. *Celtic Myth and Arthurian Romance.* New York: Columbia University Press, 1927. Attempts to find equivalents for the characters and incidents of *Sir Gawain and the Green Knight* in Celtic myth.

————. "More Celtic Elements in *Gawain and the Green Knight,*" *Journal of English and Germanic Philology,* XLII (1943), 149–184. Believes that Bercilak's girdle, the Pentangle, and "Morgne the Goddess" are derived from Celtic legends.

MARKMAN, ALAN M. "The Meaning of *Sir Gawain and the Green Knight,*" *PMLA,* LXXII (1957), 574–86. Interprets Gawain as a human hero, possessed of the qualities of the ideal medieval knight.

MOORMAN, CHARLES. "Myth and Mediaeval Literature: *Sir Gawain and the Green Knight,*" *Mediaeval Studies,* XVIII (1956), 158–172. Presents Gawain's quest as a series of moral tests.

NITZE, WILLIAM A. "Is the Green Knight Story a Vegetation Myth?" *Modern Philology,* XXXIII (1936), 351–66. Argues that the Green Knight represents the annual death and rebirth of the embodied vital principle.

PEARSALL, DEREK A. "Rhetorical 'Descriptio' in *Sir Gawain and the Green Knight,*" *Modern Language Review,* L(1955), 129–234. Discusses the poet's use of conventional medieval methods of description.

RANDALL, DALE B. J. "A Note on Structure in *Sir Gawain and the Green Knight,*" *Modern Language Notes,* LXXII (1957), 161–63. Sketches a pattern of incidents in the poem.

————. "Was the Green Knight A Fiend?" *Studies in Philology,* LVII

(1960), 479–91. Asserts that the poem may be the story of the testing of a Christian knight by a "fende" from hell.

SCHNYDER, HANS. *Sir Gawain and the Green Knight: An Essay in Interpretation.* Basel, Switzerland: Francke Verlag Bern, 1961. Uses exegetical methodology to support a multi-level Christian interpretation.

SMITHERS, G. V. "What *Sir Gawain and the Green Knight* is About," *Medium Aevum*, XXXII (1963), 171–89. Treats the poem as a religious quest testing Gawain against Christian rather than against knightly standards.

SPEIRS, JOHN. *Medieval English Poetry: The Non-Chaucerian Tradition.* London: Faber and Faber, 1957. Finds the core of the poem in ancient British pagan myths.

WATSON, M. R. "The Chronology of *Sir Gawain and the Green Knight*," *Modern Language Notes*, LXIV (1949), 85–86. Argues that the poet telescopes the third and fourth days of the Christmas festival.

ZIMMER, HEINRICH. *The King and the Corpse: Tales of the Soul's Conquest of Evil.* Bollingen Series XI. Washington: Pantheon Books, 1948. Approaches the poem from a mythic and psychiatric point of view.

Index

143

DATE DUE

OCT 23 '73	NOV 7 73		
GAYLORD			PRINTED IN U.S.A.